BEYOND THE BULLDOZER

Beyond the Bulldozer

*Ken Coates
and Richard Silburn*

Department of Adult Education, University of Nottingham

Published in 1980 by Department of Adult Education,
University of Nottingham, 14-22 Shakespeare Street,
Nottingham.

Copyright © Ken Coates and Richard Silburn, 1980,
all rights reserved.

Printed by the Russell Press Ltd., Nottingham.

Contents

	Introduction	7
I	The Problems of Slum Clearance	9
II	St Ann's on the Eve of Redevelopment	15
III	Redevelopment and Relocation	25
IV	The Experience of Rehousing: Bricks and Mortar	51

    1. The Experience of Rehousing   56
    2. The New House   62
    3. Shops, Work and Schools   69
    4. The New District: General Reactions   73

V   Family, Neighbourhood and Community   79

    1. New Districts and Old: Family Life   79
    2. Friends and Neighbours   90
    3. Formal Networks   98

VI   Money Problems   101

    1. Attitudes to Income and Wealth   101
    2. Trade Union Members and Community Attitudes   108
    3. Ownership of Consumer Durables   110

VII   The Virtues of Council Housing   116
        Appendix: The Conduct of the Surveys   125
        Acknowledgments   132

List of Tables

III:1	Acreage, Population and Provision of Dwellings in the New St. Ann's	33
III:2	Comparison of initial Population and overspill figures	33
IV:1	"How does this house compare with the house you lived in on .... Street in St. Ann's?"	63
IV:2	"How does your present house compare for access with that you lived on .... Street in St. Ann's?"	69
IV:3	"What do you think of the district as a place to live?"	74
IV:4	"How does this district compare with the old St. Ann's?"	75
V:1	Frequency of Family Contact	82
VI:1	"Do you think wages should be more equal?"	105
VI:2	Top People's Pay	106
VI:3	Households with certain goods (%)	114
VII:1	Council House Sales 1970-8	119

Introduction

In 1967 and 1968 the present authors were involved in an extended project with a group of adult students organised under the auspices of the University of Nottingham's Adult Education Department and the Worker's Educational Association. This group conducted a survey of poverty, deprivation and morale in the St Ann's area of the City of Nottingham, at that time scheduled for demolition.

In 1976, an attempt was made to seek out and interview again all those who had helped by answering a battery of detailed questions during the earlier investigation. In the event, not all could be found, and not all those found could be reinterviewed. Some older people had died, some younger ones had moved away, and some could simply not be traced. For those who wish to have more detail on these matters we have provided a brief account of them below on page 125.

In spite of these difficulties, many people were successfully discovered and did once again endure prolonged enquiries. However, since the numbers involved differed from those of 1967-8, we had to recalculate retrospectively the earlier findings of our first survey, as they applied to those to whom we were able to speak again in 1976. We discuss the degree of coincidence between these recalculated findings and our initial sample later in this report, but readers who have followed our earlier accounts must be warned at the beginning that the "1967" figures of the monograph have not been simply transposed from the earlier studies.

Whilst the University has given us every possible help and encouragement in the work of this investigation, we must naturally claim sole responsibility for any opinions or judgements which have been drawn from the data here accumulated. Opinion inside the University is as broadly-based as that outside it, and we hope to profit from the critical reactions of our colleagues as well as those of the general public.

I The Problems of Slum Clearance

Throughout the period since the Second World War, housing has been a major preoccupation of domestic social policy-makers, which has been shared by an ever-growing group of scholars and professionals. As a result there has grown up a substantial literature which documents and comments on those shifts of emphasis and direction which have been so marked a characteristic of post-war housing policy, and considers many of the wider social implications of housing and planning matters.

Much of this literature has highlighted the permanently destructive effects housing and redevelopment schemes can have upon those communities affected by them. Long-established patterns of friendship and familiarity between neighbours are upset; ties of family and kinship (which, for many, still play an important part in solving the problems of daily life) are broken; sentiments of attachment and loyalty, parish patriotism based upon family histories and personal experiences over a long period, and a capacity to identify closely with both a neighbourhood and its people are shattered and are not easily, if at all, recreated.

The earliest, and still the best-known English study is the 1956 enquiry by Young and Willmott on *Family and Kinship in East London,* a work that continues to stimulate discussion, and which marks a milestone in the record of post-war social investigation in Britain.[1] Based upon an examination of family and kinship relationships in Bethnal Green, Young and Willmott's book emphasises that "when the town planners have set themselves to create communities anew as well as homes, they have still put their faith in buildings . . . But there is surely more to a community than that. The sense of loyalty to each other amongst the inhabitants of a place like Bethnal Green is not due to buildings. It is due far more to ties of kinship and friendship which connect the *people* of one household to the *people* of another". This general point has often been re-echoed, to the point where Gans has written that "the critique of relocation has become part of the conventional wisdom of the planning and housing professions".[2]

It is, at this early point, worth noting that the Young and Willmott enquiry was carried out several years before slum-clearance became the main housing priority. The Bethnal Green that they investigated was an inner-city area that had been devastated by war-time bombing and the reallocation of population that took place was more a response to the housing crisis precipitated by the war, than it was a result of deliberate and premeditated social policy.

But whatever these far-sighted social investigators put into their critiques, the British authorities were slow to respond to the message, so much so that the first hint of official understanding did not come until 1966, with the publication of the Deeplish study.[3] This monitored an important experiment in "selective renewal" as an alternative to demolition: resources were made available to improve not only housing amenities themselves but also the surrounding environment. The reactions of the residents of Deeplish to these changes in their area were recorded, and the subsequent reports stimulated discussion and controversy among practical policy-makers and academics alike. But even while the argument about housing improvement as a strategy was germinating, the very age and decrepitude of the housing stock in a large number of industrial centres meant that whole tracts of cheap housing were rapidly and irreversibly drifting into dereliction.[4]

Housing rehabilitation can never be a universal panacea: but even where it presents an entirely relevant option, it needs to be taken up a decade *before* collapse becomes imminent, and not five years after structural deterioration has become acute. Of course, dogma may have played its part in some quarters: some local politicians may have seen clearance as a form of municipal machismo. But ultimately it was for the eminently practical reason that whole districts were literally falling to pieces, that the 1960s became a period of large-scale slum clearance schemes. These were pursued with almost ruthless vigour by the local authorities of many of our larger cities: a vigour which was matched only by the heart-searching (about alternative strategies for coping with the housing problems) on the part of community-centred social workers and activists, and by some architects and planners.

One major redevelopment scheme, indeed one of the largest and most ambitious in the British Isles, was focused on the St. Ann's district of Nottingham. A neglected and congested area of some 10,000 Victorian houses in various stages of decay and collapse, St. Ann's was demolished between the late sixties and the mid-seventies and a large estate of 3,500 new council houses has since been built on the cleared land. A detailed description and discussion about St. Ann's immediately prior to its demolition can be found in our earlier studies to which the present work is in some senses a sequel and an epilogue.[5]

From the outset the redevelopment was a controversial proposal, about which many people and groups sincerely disagreed. The viewpoint represented by the City Council among others, was that St. Ann's was so overcrowded, and the houses were, in the main, in such poor structural condition and so lacking in basic and essential amenities that demolition was a responsible act of social hygiene from which everyone would ultimately benefit. Others argued that large-scale demolition involved social costs (in terms of lost community spirit and values) which were hard to measure precisely, but would certainly outweigh the advantages that would accrue from a qualitatively improved housing stock. For this group, a programme of rehabilitation and improvement of existing stock was preferable.[6] This would go a long way to meet the "hygienic" arguments but would spare the inhabitants of St. Ann's from the fate so eloquently described and criticised by Herbert Gans. "Entire neighbourhoods have frequently been destroyed, uprooting people who had lived there for decades, closing down their institutions, mining small businesses by the hundreds, and scattering families and friends all over the city. By removing the structure of social and emotional support provided by the neighbourhood, and by forcing people to rebuild their lives separately and amid strangers elsewhere, slum clearance has often come as a serious psychological as well as financial cost to its supposed beneficiaries".[7]

Precisely the same thoughts occurred to some people in St. Ann's before the redevelopment, and were ably voiced by one sensitive outsider, Ray Gosling: "Not everybody wishes to rise with the modern world. This standard takes no account of a wish element: the wish of old people who have grown with a home and do not want to leave, cannot stand even the disturbance that reconditioning entails; who want to stay in a home where their savings are invested. And not all who do want a modern home want to spend the money: and not all can".[8]

Whatever the merits of these arguments, about which, in any particular case, honest people may disagree, the original redevelopment proposals were put into effect, albeit with changes. Now that the programme of demolition is complete, and the reconstruction very far advanced, it has become necessary for someone to describe what actually happened to the people of St. Ann's themselves, and to see how far their hopes and fears were realised, as well as evaluating the more optimistic hopes of the planners and the ambivalences and fears of the various spokesmen for the residents.

Footnotes

1. First published in 1957 by Routledge and Kegan Paul, and then revised in an edition by Pelican Books, which has been frequently reprinted since its appearance in 1962. The most extended discussion is by Jennifer Platt: *Social Research in Bethnal Green,* MacMillan, 1971.
2. Herbert Gans: *People and Plans,* Basic Books 1968, p.204.
3. Ministry of Housing: *The Deeplish Study: Improvement Possibilities in a district of Rochdale,* HMSO, 1966.
4. See Shelter: *Slum Clearance,* London, 1974. Department of Environment: *House Condition Survey,* 1971. John English, Ruth Madigan and Peter Norman: *Slum Clearance,* Croom Helm, 1976.
5. *St. Ann's: Poverty, Deprivation and Morale in a Nottingham Community,* Nottingham University, Department of Adult Education, 1967, 1968. *The Morale of the Poor,* Nottingham University, Department of Adult Education, 1968. *Poverty: The Forgotten Englishmen,* Penguin Books, 1970, and subsequently.
6. The main focus of this argument was provided by three planners, Messrs. Davis, Strickland and Wilson, at an exhibition in Nottingham City Architect's Department, July 1967.
7. Gans, *op.cit.,* p.263.
8. Ray Gosling: *St. Ann's,* Nottingham Civic Society, 1967.

II St. Ann's on the Eve of Redevelopment

The St. Ann's redevelopment area extended over some 340 acres, close to the city centre of Nottingham. Before demolition began, it contained almost ten thousand houses, crowding along cobbled streets at densities which varied to allow for different types of terraces, but which averaged 40 houses per acre. Just as the degree of concentration differed from one street to another, or even from parts of one street to adjacent parts, so also the standards of upkeep of properties, and indeed the original standards of construction, were not by any means entirely uniform.

Jumbled up among the houses were factories, shops, pubs, churches, and other industrial, commercial and recreational premises, from tiny backyard workshops and modest street-corner shops, to substantial five-storey factory buildings and large high-street shops (although none so large as the department stores to be found in the City centre itself), from small club-rooms and public halls, to a neighbourhood cinema and a public dancehall (both of which became in the last years of the old St. Ann's, and remain in the now otherwise rebuilt St. Ann's, bingo clubs). The district had originally been built, speculatively, in the building boom of the late 19th century, and, apart from one thin line of large detached houses overlooking a tree-lined pedestrian throughway, was essentially a district for the housing of Nottingham's industrial working-class, many of whom sought and found work in the shops and factories within St. Ann's itself or in the nearby Lace Market, a district of tenement factories.

While St. Ann's was no doubt a very reasonable working-class housing area by late Victorian standards, it was, by the 1960s, a largely decrepit area, in which considerable tracts of dwellings could only be described as slums, and in which both the physical condition of the houses themselves and the state of repair of such vital social amenities as sewers and drains had entered into the stage of steep decline. In the 1961 Census, the density of population in the City of Nottingham was recorded as 17 per acre. That of St. Ann's Ward (which was only part of the overall area of St. Ann's itself) was 62.2 per acre. In the City as a whole, 5.6% of persons lived at densities greater than 1½ to a room: in the Market and St. Ann's Wards respectively this proportion was 13.9% and 9.9%.[1]

The impact of such area averages, striking as they are, is however, misleading: it conceals as much as it reveals of the realities of life. St Ann's had large numbers of dwellings which were not overcrowded but which were underoccupied. For example, elderly or widowed ladies might occupy a house with as many as three bedrooms while at the same time a family of six or seven people next door might well be cramped even if the whole house was usable. Often, where houses viewed from the street might seem identical, they might in fact differ considerably internally: some of the rooms might well be uninhabitable.

Part of the difficulty of modern living in St. Ann's was a result of the unavoidable structural inadequacies of the old housing: 91% of the houses had outdoor lavatories only; 85% lacked bathrooms; 54% were without any hot water system. But at the same time, the very age of (inadequately built) houses became an increasingly insurmountable obstacle to effective repairs. Rot, damp, and collapse were widespread: many of the floors were laid directly on the earth: standards of privacy were grossly inadequate, with partition walls between houses transmitting every sound from the neighbours with random impartiality. Even where the deterioration of the fabric of a house had been arrested by careful repair, the rooms were small, and the kitchen miniscule: there was certainly no room for the installation of the batteries of consumer durables which have become a standard expectation on modern estates.

Such difficulties made life acutely hard in a number of ways. Infections spread easily, and the diseases most clearly associated with environmental poverty were widespread — bronchitis, other chest ailments in both young and old, arthritis, rheumatism and similar muscular ills among the middle-aged. Infestation problems, such as nits, were far more common in St. Ann's schools than elsewhere, and harder to eradicate permanently. Among older people, damp and cold took their toll, and arthritis and related complaints were particularly common. All these disorders were aggravated by material want among a high proportion of the residents, and by an overall lack of amenities such as playspace, green areas, trees, up-to-date facilities for community activities, and similar social investments. The schools were old and dingy, and difficult to adapt to the purposes of modern pedagogy.

Thus, by the early 1960s, and indeed well before then, St. Ann's had fallen into an unhappy state. Partly through neglect and lack of timely maintenance, partly through a natural, and not always remediable, obsolescence, and partly because general housing and other social expectations were changing to become more demanding, St. Ann's declined both in the physical sense of continuous decay, and in the social sense of a diminishing reputation and status. Some residents, among those who could afford to, got out, and bought or rented houses in newer, more esteemed suburbs; many young couples served their time on the council housing waiting-lists and eventually made their homes on one or other of the council's housing estates. Their homes in St. Ann's were quickly reoccupied by newcomers to the district, often newcomers to the City. Sometimes these newcomers came to Nottingham from other parts of the United Kingdom, such as the North-East, Liverpool and Scotland, looking for work in the very varied and, at the time, relatively buoyant

East Midlands economy. Sometimes they came from overseas. There was a colony of Italians, some of whom were ex-prisoners of war who remained, while others were attracted in the early 'fifties by the offer of work in the local coal-mines (an offer which was abruptly withdrawn before any of the migrants actually took up such employment). There were also substantial numbers of Poles who had reached the Midlands as members of the exiled Free Polish Forces, and who remained in the Midlands after the war ended: they were joined in the post-war years by smaller colonies of refugees from the Baltic States. From the mid-'fifties onwards, substantial numbers of commonwealth immigrants from the Caribbean and then the Indian sub-continent began to arrive.[2] In short, while the fabric of St. Ann's housing was slowly ageing and rotting, so the once-homogeneous social composition of its population was becoming more varied, more cosmopolitan and more changeable. Homogeneity and stability gradually gave way to mixture and turbulence, a process of change in the social neighbourhood which sometimes attracted as much local comment, as did the (to an outsider) more visible and obvious housing decay. We say "to an outsider" because more than once it was made clear to us that where people were living, day by day, amid crumbling terraces and broken yards, they came to adopt a stoical attitude to the hardship involved, a bit like those who endured the blitz. To see the area through the eyes of strangers, where that became possible, could be a painful wrench.

During the first enquiries in St. Ann's in 1967, it was the physical decay and dereliction which provoked the most sustained and vociferous criticism from the residents. This criticism amounted to a formidable rejection of the old St. Ann's.

What emerged was a widespread, longstanding and growing dissatisfaction with the area and a long list of detailed complaints about it. For example, when asked in the most general terms what they thought of St. Ann's as a place in which to live, over a quarter of the sample expressed great dissatisfaction, and fewer than 40% had anything more positive than neutral feelings towards the area. When we asked for more detailed and precise complaints we were soon able to catalogue a forbiddingly long list of grievances, most of which focused on aspects of the physical decay of the neighbourhood. Thus the damp and the disrepair of particular houses, combined with the overall decrepitness of the district was mentioned, often with great emphasis, by 25% of all those interviewed, half of whom went on to mention in detail the squalor which made housekeeping and child-rearing especially difficult. Moreover, the problems of dirt, dust and smoke, sometimes aggravated by the arrival of vermin, grew steadily more unbearable as the physical demolition itself got underway. There were times when the entire district seemed to be lying under a thick haze of brickdust, kippering in the smell and smoke from endlessly burning floor-timbers and debris, as house after house fell to the bulldozers.

Rubble became a natural habitat, and a nightmarish environment in which to pass the months or years of patient waiting before your own row of houses was cleared.

It was also apparent that the acute difficulties of living in such an unpromising physical environment put an increasing strain upon personal relationships, both within families and between families. We discovered a painful and inexorable erosion of neighbourly sentiment as people started to criticise one another for the dirt in the streets and yards, and again the process of redevelopment aggravated many of these tensions. As the horizon opened with gaps between the terraces, so people opened their capacities for blame and recrimination. We encountered an increasing number of complaints which went beyond the uncomfortable conditions themselves to accuse the people who allegedly caused these conditions. Usually these were nameless, distant people who lived around the corner, or in the next street, whose antisocial behaviour was allegedly causing or worsening the problems of dirt and neglect, while their children were thought to be an endless source of trouble and noise. Such scapegoats, individually and jointly, were often blamed for the bad reputation the district was supposedly attracting to itself.

Set against this sorry tale of demoralisation and decay, however, we were also able to discover some of the positive qualities that people thought they would miss when they were rehoused. For every one who wanted to escape from his neighbours, there were two who thought that they would miss theirs; this should remind us how enduring were many neighbourly contacts, and how staunch they remained. All this serves to emphasise an ambiguity in people's attitudes which was clearly and frequently expressed: a mixture of irritation and exasperation on the one hand and solidarity and warmth on the other; of stern criticism, at times almost vindictive, coinciding with an immediate and generous sympathy; of regret at the decline of an old way of life, mingling with anxious curiosity about an uncertain future in a new area.

But it wasn't only the people who were to be missed. Even more frequently mentioned was the network of small corner-shops. The corner-shop played a crucial part in the life of old St. Ann's. First and foremost it was a commercial convenience; a place where one could buy an apparently infinite range of foodstuffs, pots and pans, tobacco, beer and sweets. Moreover, the small shop was almost never shut. Trading might begin as early as 6.30 or 7.00 in the morning, with fresh bread and milk and perhaps the morning paper, and would seldom close, even on a Sunday, before 9.30 or 10.00 at night. Always open, never more than a few yards away, the corner-shop was also a meeting place, an active gossip exchange, and an early warning-system. On most St. Ann's streets, little happened that was not circulating through the corner-shop grapevine within minutes, from malicious tittle-tattle about who had or had not been seen with whom, to immediate and practical concern for the old lady who hadn't collected her morning milk, or the child down with measles.

If the shops were intimate as well as small, so were the pubs: little social islands scattered all over the area. Dozens of such houses not only provided beer from the wood, instead of the plastic brews so often found in the new gin-palaces, but close conviviality and conversation in people-sized rooms, where the rubric "snug" over the door usually meant what it said.

Then there were other, less tangible, features about St. Ann's that people appreciated. Above all, it was central. No part of St. Ann's was more than three minutes walk from St. Ann's Well Road, a bustling shopping-street, and no part of St. Ann's Well Road was more than 10 minutes walk from the central area of Nottingham, from the central fruit and meat market, from the Palais de Dance, from the large showrooms and department stores of Parliament Street and the Old Market Square, from the cinemas and the services to be found in the centre of every large city. St. Ann's was also close to the flea-market at Sneinton, and to that unique district of large and small manufacturers housed in architecturally resonant if now crumbling Victorian depots and workshops in the Lace Market; manufacturers who looked to St. Ann's for a constant supply of cheap female labour, either as factory machinists or as domestic outworkers finishing lace in their own homes for rock-bottom wages.

Partly due to its own character, and partly as a result of its central position right by the heart of the City, St. Ann's had an atmosphere of its own, and many people were fully conscious of it and appreciated it. Tied up in many of the judgements people were making was the feeling that nowhere else was, or could be, quite the same, that St. Ann's had an especial feel about it that could not easily be imitated or replaced.

In short, then, our enquiries in 1967 and 1968, when ultimate redevelopment was talked about everywhere, revealed that those who were shortly to leave the district had a complicated but clear set of feelings and reactions which included an emphatic rejection of their physical surroundings, but a strong sensitivity to some of the characteristics of the neighbourhood that distinguished it from other parts of Nottingham; the wish to escape from the growing squalor mingled with a certain rather marked apprehension about how to establish roots in some quite new area of the City.

How did these people fare in the change? It was this question which we set out to answer in our follow-up enquiry. But before we consider their reactions to the move, after resettlement, we must first look at the actual process of clearance, as it affected people during the time between our 1967-8 survey and the later investigation of 1976.

Footnotes

1. The evidence on this matter is presented in our *St. Ann's: Poverty, Deprivation and Morale in a Nottingham Community,* pp.25-8.
2. Further information on immigrant communities may be found in Elizabeth Burney: *Housing on Trial,* Oxford University Press, 1967, pp.179, et seq, and Daniel Lawrence: *Black Migrants – White Natives,* Cambridge University Press, 1974.

III Redevelopment and Relocation

To judge simply by the publicity documents and announcements that commonly accompany a major scheme of public rehousing, such as that of St. Ann's, the whole proceeding is a complex, expensive, time-consuming but nonetheless rational and orderly process of decision-making and administrative action, involving local politicians and administrators, planning and housing officials, local Treasury officers, contracted building firms, and a legion of sub-contractors, all working together in concert with their Whitehall and central governmental counterparts. Every one of these experts are, it seems, animated by a selfless concern with the public interest in general and that of the directly affected population in particular. Thus, a model of the assumptions which underlie a clearance scheme such as that of St. Ann's might be the following carefully structured system.

a. That the properties to be demolished are of uniformly poor design or structural condition so that demolition is an act of social cleanliness;

b. that they will be replaced, on the cleared site, by new houses of superior design or specification;

c. that, subject to necessary overspill to reduce overall population densities to more acceptable levels, the tenants and residents of the clearance area will be rehoused in the new houses, or at the least, have an option to be so re-housed;

d. to this end, in the post-Skeffington era of attempts at public consultation and participation in the planning processes, the residents in a clearance area should be able to play some real part in determining the character and design of the new estate;

e. that the scheme, when complete, will have materially improved the housing standards of the affected population, while doing minimum violence to the valuable networks of informal contacts that give a neighbourhood character and meaning.

What this model, and the public documents and announcements, fail to mention are some of the less tidy factors, less disinterested elements that play a crucial (and not always dishonourable) part in the process of decision making and implementation. Local party political rivalries, at the level of City Hall and higher up; personal political ambitions and animosities; the Byzantine complexities of status and hierarchy between one local authority department and another; established and nascent links between public authorities and local and national commercial interests, patterns of collaboration and tension between local officials and their ministerial opposite numbers; the interplay between all these agencies and those individuals and groups which claim to represent some or all of the citizenry at large: these and many other well-concealed cross-currents of ambition and interest all serve to make sure that the practicalities of a major rehousing scheme are seldom clear-cut, logical, rational, and free of personal and private interest. An attempt to reconstruct the "natural history" of the St. Ann's scheme, which, no matter how closely-researched must still remain incomplete, nonetheless throws into relief some of these complexities.

Needless to say, one would hardly expect a scheme as grandiose as that of the St. Ann's redevelopment to proceed in an unaltered, unalterable form from the first draft blueprint to emerge from the planners' studies. In any major redevelopment, proposals will be amended in detail, or indeed in principle, in response to events and experience. If such amendments are the result of popular reactions, complaints, and suggestions, we may well think "so much the better". But if they leave democratic pressures unsatisfied, and have no beneficial impact on the problems identified by residents and potential residents, then they may well be differently evaluated.

It is always difficult to plan accurately, and fractionally more so if one works in a framework of inadequate consultation. On the other hand, if the plans are to be modified sharply, if drastic twists and turns in public policy are likely, even unavoidable, then the less consultation the better, from the point of view of some kinds of planner.

What changes the eye doesn't see, such changes the heart doesn't grieve about. The record of the planners of the new St. Ann's was certainly not devoid of changes: altered targets, modified decisions about land use, mutations in housing standards; and viewed retrospectively it all looks a bit like one of those terrifying switchbacks which used to be a necessary amenity in every major pleasure ground. Parts of the switchback resulted from a negative form of consultation, in that popular protest sometimes deflected officialdom from its original choices: but most of it grew, like Topsy, within the administrative difficulties of so large an operation.

In May 1967, the City Planning Department published a pleasantly illustrated pamphlet called *St. Ann's — Towards Renewal.* The pictures were carefully selected, showing the cobbled streets as clean as they had ever been, and a great deal cleaner than they usually were at the material time in question; and making the most of every captive green frond that had accidently survived in that largely urban desert. But the text was more interesting. Under the heading "Principles for Renewal" we find a plain statement of what the original plan was intended to bring about. Surprisingly, the first of these principles began with the rubric "Road Proposals". The major roads, we were told

> "will be the proposed Eastern Bypass and Carlton Road which form part of the primary network for the City."

What this means, at its simplest, is that the most crucial decisions about land-usage in St. Ann's had already been taken, before housing redevelopment was more than a gleam in a councillor's eye, and had been outlined in an earlier document published by the City Engineers' Department in 1966, called *A Traffic Plan for the City 1965-2005*. This barbaric set of proposals was a road-traffic plan for the entire city, inspired largely by the 1962 Buchanan Report on Traffic in Towns. For St. Ann's the traffic proposals included two major trunk roads which would have neatly divided the area into four separate parts. These would have been extensively bridged and furnished with subways, we were informed. Part of the bypass itself would be tunnelled. Nonetheless "major road junctions are planned at the intersections of the proposed Eastern Bypass and St. Ann's Well Road". The Eastern Bypass, elevated on stilts, was to have roared across the lovely old Arboretum gardens, and once it had desecrated that quiet area and rolled on it would have been a veritable urban motorway searing through the new estates. Some members of the Architect's staff were appalled at this prospect, and did everything possible to oppose it. Their arguments about noise-levels were all over-ruled, and they sometimes gave their explanations for this in uncharitable terms, since they believed that the material planning considerations were running a bad second to the pecking order in the Chief Officers' ranks, and that their (junior) department therefore could not ever win an argument with the more senior planners of highways from the City Engineer's Department. It was not because of the sound advice of socially conscious designers and architects, however, that this monstrous nostrum was finally ended: on the contrary, the municipality had to be over-ruled by ministerial authority before it could be stopped. The Great Eastern Bypass was finally killed, by the order of the Minister in Whitehall. Thus it seems that it was no innocent quirk of planners' jargon that led into the new proposals with an announcement about the road framework, but that in fact this seeming illogicality was a direct reflection of the priorities as they emerged from within the local power structure.

Despite the ultimate triumph of common-sense in relation to unwanted motorways, it remained the case that the greater part of the physical design of the new St. Ann's had to acknowledge this proposed road-system. Indeed, to this day, parts of the pathway intended for the Bypass are still clearly visible as a broad tract of open land, overgrown with willow-herb and luxuriant weeds. In some places, handy bridges and tunnelled subways ease the path of residents from one side of this unintended nature conservancy to the other.

In *second* place among the "Principles" came the subtitle: "Living". This was about housing and related amenities:

"The housing areas should be developed with the ultimate aim of locating modern homes in pleasant surroundings. Pedestrians will be separated from motor cars in their movement around the area, and the motorist will have adequate garaging and parking facilities. Play areas, open spaces and associated housing uses including pubs, clubs and community buildings will be included within the plan.

> To provide improved living conditions and because of the need to allow for the ancillary uses mentioned above, together with schools and industrial re-location, it is anticipated that the existing population of some 30,000 will be reduced by about one-third."

This very early statement of intentions, then, anticipated an overspill of about 10,000 people who would have to be rehoused on other estates elsewhere within the authority's boundaries. Now of course, as the pamphlet rightly stresses, any redevelopment which replaces cramped terraces with larger houses, small back-yards with modest front and rear gardens, Victorian school-buildings with airy and open-plan schools surrounded by playing-fields, any such redevelopment will necessarily involve some relocation of overspill population. The proportion will vary from one scheme to another, and the figure of 30% would fall very much within the expected range. However, the estimate of 30% turned out to be only the first of a series of ever-increasing figures. Already by 1968 the Report of the Chief Planning Officer had raised the estimated overspill population to 17,700, or 59% of the original population. So large an increase might well have led to a considerably more agitated public discussion than in fact took place. Debate, indeed scrutiny, of this and other important issues was, however, considerably muted by the timely introduction of a new municipal convention. City Council reports, even those of the utmost public importance and widespread public concern, began to carry the underlined front page heading "CONFIDENTIAL. Not to be released to the press without authority (C) (date) Nottingham Corporation". It may be doubted whether the intention of the pioneers of copyright law was to prevent municipal secrets from escaping into the view of the electors and ratepayers, but be that as it may, it was under this restriction that the November 1969 *Report of the City Planning Officer on Future Population in St. Ann's* was placed before the councillors.[1]

This does not assume a population reduction of "about one third" or even 59%. Perhaps it should speak for itself:

> "The population of the St. Ann's area at the commencement of redevelopment was approximately 30,000. Based on the assumptions in Table 5, the initial figure population is estimated to be in the order of 10,500 and this would result in an 'overspill' of about 19,500 people which is 1,800 greater than in the report of 1968. However, taking into account the natural increase in population, it is estimated that the future population that will be accommodated in the redevelopment area could rise to above 12,000. In order to accommodate the additional overspill it would be necessary to provide about 670 dwellings outside the St. Ann's redevelopment area, that is approximately 84 per year during the course of the eight years during which clearance has been or will be taking place. This, of course, would tend to increase the demand for corporation building outside the redevelopment areas and advance the date when the corporation's available building land becomes exhausted. To date, about 6,500 persons living in St. Ann's have already been rehoused."

The Table here cited is reproduced below, together with a further table from the same source which renders the whole matter quite transparent.

Table III:1.
Acreage, Population and Provision of Dwellings in the new St. Ann's (Estimates)*

Phase	Net Residential Acreage	Density b.p.a.	Estimated Population	Estimated Dwellings
1	24.5	80	1370	510
2	25.5	80	1430	530
3	14.4	75	760	280
4	13.6	75	710	260
5	10.2	)	530	200
6	21.0	)	1100	410
7	13.3	75)	700	260
8	11.2	)	580	220
9	21.2	)	1110	410
10	15.6	)	820	300
11	7.8	)	410	150
Sub-Total	178.3		9520	3530
Less Contingencies	5.5	75	320	100
Sub-Total	172.8	—	9200	3430
Add population and housing to be retained			1300	430
Total			10500	3860

Table III:2.
Comparison of initial Population and overspill figures

	1967 Report	1968 Report	1969 Report
Estimated Population	19,000	12,300	10,500
Estimated Overspill	11,000	17,700	19,500

*This table is Table 5 in Nottingham Corporation's November 1969 *Report.*

In a nutshell, the overspill estimate in 1969 was increased once again, this time to 65%, almost twice the proportion of two years earlier.

This figure of 65% overspill is repeated in the Nottinghamshire County Council's Structure Plan, where we are told in the *Draft Report of Survey* that

> "in St. Ann's only about 35% of the original 10,000 or so dwellings are likely to be replaced."

indicating a population of some nine and a half thousand. Finally, a further statement in the *Revised Draft Written Statement* of 1977 seems to indicate that 3,500 will be the total number of dwellings, which would now include the total of older (reprieved) houses, which are featured separately in the 1969 report of the City Council.

All of these estimates, however, are official calculations of the size of an existing population, and the likely size of a future population. The actual proportion of St. Ann's residents who were either rehoused elsewhere, or whose death or departure removed them from the housing lists altogether, turned out, as closely as we can judge, to be even higher than these estimates. Of the 141 families whom we traced in 1976, all of whom had been rehoused by the Council, only 25% were living in the new St. Ann's. The reasons for this final discrepancy are not hard to discover. Houses in the new St. Ann's were not allocated only to residents from the demolition area; some appear to have been allocated to families in need from the housing waiting-list, while others seem to have gone to existing council tenants whose move into St. Ann's vacated another (perhaps older and cheaper) council house elsewhere in the City. In this way the number of new houses available for the population of the old St. Ann's was further eroded.

This very high overspill fraction, necessary, indeed inevitable as it may have been if the new St. Ann's was to be a tolerable place to live, does have a number of planning implications. One of these relates to the necessary processes of consultation, that should both precede and follow through any significant scheme of public rehousing. In the early stages of planning, it may well be possible to indicate what proportion of those living in a redevelopment area might expect to be moved elsewhere, but of course the practical and specific decisions about who stays and who leaves can only be taken very much later. Even then, such decisions are commonly made in a relatively random and spasmodic way. The most minimal public participation in planning decision-taking would challenge this: elaborate general consultations with the public at large should surely begin with enquiries about who is anxious to leave the district, followed by queries about who is prepared to leave. If some progress can be made at this initial stage, then a start will have been made towards identifying those who need to be consulted at a later stage about the detailed proposals for redevelopment as possible future residents.

Furthermore, this initial screening-operation may not be as hard to mount as it might appear to be. Nor is the affected population likely to be as uniformly hostile to all proposals for change as some slum-sentimentalists have alleged. On the contrary, a number of surveys from different parts of the country suggest first that significant proportions of a local population faced with redevelopment are pleased at the prospect, and secondly that large numbers of them, if given the chance, are prepared to leave the district altogether (i.e. to become part of an overspill population). Reviewing this evidence *English, Madigan and Norman* argue thus:

"The typical pattern of response in a poor condition inner city area would be between one quarter and one-third of households in favour of staying put, one quarter to one-third in favour of a change of accommodation within the same locality and between one-third and one-half of households in favour of a complete change of both houses and locality".[2] This summary certainly corresponds to what we know of the attitude of the St. Ann's population. A survey carried out by the Housing Department in 1967, fairly early on in the planning stage, showed that 38% of households would prefer to be rehoused elsewhere than in St. Ann's. Our own 1968 enquiry produced a figure of 47%. Moreover, it is more than likely that this figure would steadily increase, as living conditions changed from disgracefully bad to absolutely intolerable whilst the work of demolition got under way.

These, however, are not necessarily the main reproaches which people would make against planners, long-suffering though those who live through slum-clearance commonly have to be. Essentially what such a resident wants to know, as quickly and as definitely as is possible, is when he can expect to move, and to where. Unfortunately, prompt and precise answers are seldom forthcoming to so blunt a question. For a start the bureaucratic processes that accompany a redevelopment scheme are painstaking, time-consuming and subject to unforeseen reversals, necessitating modification to plans already announced. For example no redevelopment at all can start before the permission to proceed has been granted. This will not normally be granted until there has been a public enquiry. The enquiry cannot take place until the local authority has established what properties it wishes to purchase compulsorily. The authority cannot make and justify these decisions until the Public Health Authority has inspected all properties for fitness. These initial stages can be expected to take many months, during which bemused but expectant residents will be called upon by Inspectors and officials from several local authority departments, examining for fitness, establishing tenure, canvassing for housing preferences and so forth. The ordinary resident, ignorant of these necessary stages, may be forgiven at first for supposing that the arrival of an official of the local authority heralds imminent action, but he quickly learns that it heralds little more than the imminent arrival of sundry other officials of the local authority. The better-informed, but by now equally bemused resident, who appreciates the slow mechanics of compulsory purchase, may well have read one of the cleverly-designed progress reports issued periodically by the Planning Department. In May 1970, for example, he may have obtained a copy of *St. Ann's: Renewal in Progress*. On page 16, he will have studied a map and a timetable. He will have observed that the redevelopment was planned in 11 phases. First, if everything went according to plan, emptying the properties prior to demolition and rehousing the residents of Phase 1 should have begun in the Spring of 1968. The building programme in that phase should be completed three and a bit years later in the Summer of 1971 when the first new houses would be ready for letting. By that Summer of 1971 rehousing of residents would have begun in all subsequent phases up to Phase 8, and presumably would have been completed in all phases up to Phase 4 at least, as building in that zone was planned to start during the Winter of 1970/71. Residents in the final phases 10 and 11 would have to wait until the second half of 1972 before their rehousing would begin, by which times building would be finished on Phases 1 and 2, and should be substantially finished in Phases 3 and 4. Building on the last phases would be complete by Autumn 1976, again if everything went according to plan. It is clear from this timetable that the overwhelming majority of residents in the first phases would of necessity be rehoused elsewhere in the City. It would take about three years before new houses would become available in St. Ann's, and it was anticipated that a substantial part of the district would have been knocked down within those three years, and the dispossessed tenants found living-space elsewhere. Whatever a tenant's views about that, and no matter how closely he had grasped the logic of the phasing, he would still experience further considerable confusion, because of the sub-phasing within each major phase. And then, for reasons good and bad, the sequence of phasing could be disrupted and modified. Even the most persistent student of redevelopment could be baffled subsequently to discover that, say, demolition within phases which were intended to be later, in fact preceded others which had been marked up as "earlier".

The less persistent student, content to wait patiently for his turn, could be inconvenienced and sometimes angered by the consequences of such apparently minor modifications. We heard, on more than one occasion, of families who had been assured of imminent rehousing subsequently being told of a further prolonged delay, while others who had been told to expect considerable delay, were suddenly required to leave within a few days. Experiences of this kind, exaggerated and multiplied by backyard gossip and rumour, served to notch up even further (and often, it appears, unnecessarily) the anxieties and tensions that must always surround the prospect of compulsorily moving house.

So much for the official side of the problem of participation. But what of the worm's eye view?

"You can't get to know anything at all". That was the constant complaint while people were awaiting demolition, and this was beyond doubt the major impediment to effective community responses, whether organised formally or informally.

"I was at the greengrocers a fortnight ago", said one lady who talked to us at length. "There was a woman there, and she says 'Yes', she says, 'I do want to move, but', she says, 'they came on Monday and I've got to be out by Saturday'. Now that's what I don't want". Tales and rumours of this kind were a frequent and persistent theme in the St. Ann's back-yard grapevine. Reliable information was always in short supply, and it was seldom that the official and semi-official networks were able to provide up-to-date information of sufficient detail to counter the force of rumour. One such semi-official grouping was SATRA, the St. Ann's Tenants' and Residents' Association, which tried to represent some of the inhabitants during the long ordeal of clearance, and undoubtedly met a whole series of deeply felt needs for that part of the affected population. Although this association was not narrowly partisan, and maintained fairly cordial relations with the authorities over a prolonged period, here is what one of its active supporters told us about the outcome: "We've tried to get to know all sorts of things, about how long we should be here, why they are pulling these houses down, where they're building the new houses, where the factory's going to be — and all that kind of thing. You can't get to know anything at all".

To be fair, there were answers to some of these questions, even if some of those answers changed from time to time. But there was also a considerable lag in publicising them, even though none of these matters concerned the kind of issue which is normally involved when people talk about "participation" in planning. Rather, we are looking simply at the direct personal involvement of men and women whose lives were about to be considerably and permanently changed, and who might well expect to be totally uprooted from a neighbourhood in which they had spent a lifetime. Complaints about lack of information did not reflect any preoccupation with the wider issues treated in the Skeffington Report, but were immediately centred on the most elementary requests: people wanted to know what authority intended to do with their own families, "where they intend to put us", "when we'll have to go", and so on. Far from seeking to influence official decisions for the better, such questioners were convinced that, (however capricious a planners' mind might appear to be), the one piece of information that would never affect the outcome of its labours would be the opinions of the client population.

Certainly a bewildered distrust of public authority born of rich and prolonged experience, and amounting at times to passive resignation in the face of the apparently inevitable, will inhibit purposeful community responses even from those most affected. But reactions of distrust and long-suffering are not confined to the activities of the public authorities alone. There are private, unrepresentative, powers, even more remote and capricious, to be confronted, as well as debilitating tensions generated within the community itself.

A graphic example of these is to be seen in the case of the Pie Factory. This company has become a household name, synonymous in large parts of the country with pork pies, which it manufactures to a very high standard. After the war, the factory started up, we were informed

> "on the corner of a bombed out house. Then they took another old house, and an old warehouse, and converted that into a bakehouse. Then they took another old house next door and converted that. So they took all the shops and houses down the left hand side of Alfred Street."

The pies sold well. As the factory and its ancillary shops spread out, so the numbers of employees increased. But this impromptu business was smack in the middle of a tightly cloistered residential area. The result was a painful intrusion into the lives of all its neighbours. All sorts of reproaches were easily heard wherever the sound or scent of the factory fanned out.

> "The street: it's terrible, dirty! The factory grease all over everywhere, all on the floor, running down the gutter and the pavement. The two drains at the bottom of the hill are clogged solid with congealed fat."

That was the verdict of one lady who lived nearby. Across the street from her came confirming evidence:

> "Saturday morning they just open up the doors and swill it out into the street, and get the pastry up, but all the greasy water goes down into the grates: and of course it's solid with grease."

When the drains were blocked, the streets commonly flooded, and life became very unpleasant. But this was not the only pollution hazard suffered by people living near the factory. There was also noise:

> "It must have been about 2 o'clock yesterday morning: metal trays flying about, pork pies and cakes. All the vans are steel lined, and they take these metal trays and slam them in. Bang goes the door, the engines are revving ... and then there's the smell."

Another old lady around the corner was deaf:

> "I don't hear that now, but I smell the devil of a smell early in the morning: ooh, early . . . about twoish, threeish, cooking."

However, for those not so handicapped:

> "The noise is the biggest bind. I've got a stack of letters in there: town clerk, councillors, MPs. Councillors have been to see me, the health people . . . I've walked the streets and signed petitions. I mean, this has been before a committee on the Council."

Of course, by the time Council committees were made aware of this issue, the fundamental damage had already been done. In more stringent later days, planning permission for the conversion of residential accommodation into factories is, rightly, harder to come by. During the slow decline of St. Ann's, however, this one factory regularly woke people up, night after night, for years on end. Parents complained that the recurrent noise at night was damaging their children's concentration at school, and interfering with their own health. Not one of the people living in houses nearby was without complaints: the quota of smell, pollution and general hubbub was lavishly shared around.

And yet what was actually done about it? We interviewed the treasurer of the St. Ann's Tenants' and Residents' Association (SATRA), a lively man with a young family, who lived on the edge of the affected area, which did not protect him from suffering regular disturbance from the loading vans, creating pandemonium in the small hours. He had been involved in the organisation of the petition which was mentioned in the complaint recorded above. How many signatures did they obtain? We asked, because it was clear to us that a few hundred people round and about had reasonable cause for complaint. The answer, to us, as outsiders, was staggering: "forty or so": this represented the merest handful of families, almost all, we were told later, from one street. Why had the inhabitants of other streets not joined in? The plan of the area resembled a reverse letter E, with the factory spread up along the rear of one side of the spine, and adjacent streets joining that spine at right angles. Consequently, all who lived within earshot along the facing side of the spine-road, and both sides of the branches, shared regularly in the acute inconveniences set out in the petition.

It appears that the main reason for the limited response was quite simple. On the one street lived a cluster of "respectable" families, many of them in houses which were owner-occupied, who had often worked hard to maintain their properties against all adverse pressures from the elements. In the parallel road alongside, not only were most houses rented, and consequently more run-down, but one or two were inhabited by prostitutes. Kerb-crawling cars were in a habit of cruising the district in the evenings, looking out for these ladies. The resultant tension was extreme. Girls from the "respectable" houses could not go out at night, even round the corner to the local beer-off, without running the risk of unpleasant encounters with men who were soliciting, commonly in a crudely unpleasant way, for sexual favours. Not unnaturally, the existence of even the tiniest handful of prostitutes thus produced a most vehement reaction, among their neighbours, since they were felt to imperil the standards of all who wished to be accepted as living conventionally. No one of these residents would dream of looking for joint action with nearby persons sharing this taint, so that the scope of petitions, even on matters which involved everybody, remained limited to the informal networks within which people knew and trusted one another.

This is an extreme case, and many lesser tensions divided people into groups and clusters less stridently, and maybe less permanently, than this. But it helps to explain how difficult community action can be, even in the face of the most painful provocation. It also helps to reveal some of the problems which are involved in public participation in planning: even in the most restricted meaning which can be attached to these much-abused words.

There is a long tradition which encourages advocates of democratic ideas to exempt the most depressed, most abject citizens from their healing benefit. Rousseau spoke with contempt of the "out-of-elbow rascals" who would, he thought, "have been driven with contempt from the ranks of a Roman cohort, in the days when soldiers were defenders of liberty".[3] Engels invented the nasty word *lumpenproletarian* to describe such riff-raff:

> "The scum of the depraved elements of all classes which established headquarters in the big cities, is the worst of all possible allies. This rabble is absolutely venal and absolutely brazen."[4]

Recalling such uncharitable thoughts, Norman Dennis shows that modern planning ideology has inherited a large measure of their intolerance.

"The people of Ship Street, Tally's Corner, or the Towpath" — he writes — "the sub-working class — are more likely to have passive market-research definitions of participation imposed on them by decision-takers than are citizens in other localities".[5]

This seems to be true, above all because the oppositional power of such groups is so much feebler than that of better-placed communities. If active participation is a larger and more complex aspiration than simple self-defence, it seems clear that a minimum capacity for self-defence is a precondition for any more ambitious involvement whatever.

Self-defence, however, is something which was perfectly possible in the old St. Ann's, given only a sufficiency of time in which to react.

The St. Ann's Tenants' and Residents' Association, whatever its limitations, showed real initiative and encouraged an active response on social and individual issues by those residents it was able to organise. Beginning with a general campaign on broad issues (concern to "demolish the bad, preserve the good"; to safeguard people living around derelict houses; to prevent areas adjacent to clearance zones becoming "dumping grounds" for problem families, and so on), SATRA always proclaimed an abstract desire for "popular participation in planning". Although SATRA never ceased to be actively concerned about such matters, in reality it was far more successful as an ad hoc voluntary welfare organisation than it was as an alternative planning office. Margaret Behrman, a full-time SATRA community worker told us in December 1971 that the Association was most successful in fields like the organisation of playgroups, the maintenance of citizens' advisory services, and the offering of help, particularly to old people, who needed representing in their disputes with the local authority.

True the Association gained an early victory by winning a reprieve for one condemned street, which still stands in 1979 as a witness to the good judgement of SATRA's petitioners: but following that concession, few other changes were made in the actual decisions of the planning departments, in accommodation to any popular pressures, whether from SATRA members or anyone else. Many self-corrections were made for technical reasons, or as a result of intra-departmental skirmishing, or simply because it had become evident that earlier schemes were wrong-headed. Yet, when the Ministry vetoed the planned by-pass road and one large area was therefore given to understand that its clearance might be indefinitely deferred, SATRA *was* able to organise meetings throughout that zone (Phase 10 of the overall scheme) in order to insist that its inhabitants be rehoused according to the originally promised schedule. This successful campaign proves (if proof were needed) that the people of St. Ann's were perfectly capable of defending themselves: but by the time it was undertaken, not only had all the major planning decisions already been made, and sometimes remade, without any real consultation, but a large part of the old St. Ann's population had already been rehoused, often far away from the demolition areas.

From the point of view of public participation in planning, the St. Ann's redevelopment was a dismal experience for the public. However, it was an experience from which other vigilant community groups, elsewhere in the City, learned a lot. Moreover, events gave them an early opportunity to apply their learning. Equally the local authority became somewhat more adept at observing the superficial appearances of open consultation. The occasion was the proposal to extend slum clearance and redevelopment to other decaying inner-city areas.

It was in August 1972 that the City Planning Officer embarked upon the preparation of a new scheme for widespread slum clearance in another district, the Meadows, whose inhabitants had already learned something from the treatment accorded to those living in the old St. Ann's. From the beginning MATAR (The Meadows Tenants' and Residents' Association) had not only a warning example, but also a series of successful and unsuccessful experiences to emulate or pass over.

The August 1972 surveys were sent to 100 people rehoused in the new St. Ann's, not necessarily having moved there from the old St. Ann's, since some people moved in from elsewhere: and to 100 inhabitants of the Meadows who might shortly expect to find themselves in clearance areas. Only 52% of the Meadows residents, and 45% of the St. Ann's people, responded.

The questions all concerned matters of detail. Whether gardens should be fenced or not, (95% of those answering thought they should) or whether signposting was adequate (60% of respondents among new St. Ann's dwellers thought it was not): this kind of issue was explored with helpful precision. But major questions of overall planning were not touched at all, and those issues which did emerge from the two questionnaires were not all fully reported to the appropriate committee of the Council.

If market research is the best that slum clearance populations can expect, in terms of participation, then it is clear that even that may easily fall far short of the rigorous standards applied to the promotion of a new brand of margarine, or an exotic non-nicotine-bearing cigarette. First, there will usually be rather little money available for survey purposes. Second, the customers are already guaranteed, caught and docketed, so the form of any enquiry is "which of those needs and foibles which we have agreed to recognise might we reasonably take it on ourselves to meet, other things being equal?" rather than "what must we be able to know and do in order to satisfy this customer?" Thirdly, as in the case of St. Ann's, the investigation may well be undertaken too late to permit any significant readjustment of actual plans.

The reform of local government and the development of highly qualified structure-planning teams has ensured that somewhat greater resources can be deployed by local authorities than used to be the case. It remains to be seen whether this improvement will result in any permanent betterment in communication between planners and those for whom plans are supposedly made.

Footnotes

1. It is only right and proper to point out that since the end of that conspiratorial decade, local government has become a distinctly more visible process, even if it is still far from being open enough.
2. *Slum Clearance,* Croom Helm, 1976, p.156.
3. J.J. Rousseau: *Social Contract* (1762) London. Oxford University Press, World's Classics, 1947, p.402.
4. Frederick Engels: Prefatory note 1874 to *The Peasant War in Germany* (1850) in Marx Engels Selected Works, Volume 1. Moscow: Foreign Languages Publishing House, 1958, p.646.
5. Norman Dennis: *Public Participation and Planners Blight,* Faber and Faber, 1972, p.256. We are indebted to Norman Dennis for the two preceding references.

IV The Experience of Rehousing: Bricks and Mortar

The most cursory examination of the new addresses of our original respondents made it clear that in the case of the St. Ann's redevelopment a very large population was physically uprooted and their houses torn down; most of them were rehoused elsewhere in the city, in many cases at some considerable distance away. Moreover many of the new properties constructed on the cleared sites were then let to families who had no previous links with the old St. Ann's at all, but who were drawn off the housing waiting list or who exchanged from existing council houses on other estates into one of the new properties. In other words, redevelopment involved the scattering of one population to all quarters of the wider city, and its replacement by a smaller and, in substantial measure, new population.

Now this may well mean that, at the end of the day, a set of old and inferior houses has been replaced by new houses of superior design and specification, and that most people's, if not everybody's, housing standards will be significantly improved. But it is by no means so obvious that original tenants will have had so much as an option on one of the new houses, indeed it is quite apparent that many will not. In this case considerable violence must inevitably be done to traditional and largely informal community networks both for those rehoused in some other district and for the minority who, though rehoused in the same district, find that they are living among a population, many of whom are strangers, without a shared memory, a previous loyalty to or sentiment for the district.

As we have already pointed out, the Corporation had completed a survey in 1967, in which it had asked, among other questions, where people would prefer to live after demolition. This enquiry revealed that, in the first phase of the clearance zone, 37.5% of the people did not object to "moving right away", while 20% wanted to stay "fairly near", and 42.5% wished to remain "near". Of course, none of this constituted "consultation" but it does offer a certain post hoc justification, in that the authorities had not totally mis-guessed the popular mood.

Today only one quarter of our original respondents are still living in St. Ann's; most of these are living in one of the new houses, although a tiny handful of people are living in the one or two streets on the edge of St. Ann's that were excluded from the redevelopment order in favour of rehabilitation and improvement.

One in ten of our respondents was rehoused in other central areas of the City; generally speaking they have been allocated older properties in long-established residential areas. In some cases this was to swap one slum property for another; indeed one or two of our interviews took place in houses which are already themselves condemned and scheduled for imminent demolition in fresh clearance programmes. Sometimes events outwitted us in this race against the bulldozers: one of the reasons we lost trace of some families was precisely because they had been moved to another slum property, and then been moved, or moved themselves, again. In at least three cases, when we arrived at the new address we found it boarded up ready for demolition or actually demolished.

Yet removal to an older property, even one of approximately the same period as the house vacated, is by no means always to exchange one slum for another. Far from it; there are districts fairly close to the centre of Nottingham, districts such as Sneinton or Sherwood, or parts of Radford and Forest Fields, which, though dating from the Victorian or Edwardian periods will, given careful husbandry, still have many years of life before them. Generally the houses are somewhat larger than the properties in the old St. Ann's, and were probably built with robuster materials for a generally more prosperous section of the population, as is witnessed by the decorative brickwork which frequently surrounds windows and doors. They are houses of a traditional design, and the patterned tiling of porch and hall, and the occasional stained glass above the front doors, lays claim to a Victorian sense of style which was quite absent from the functional boxes of the poorer terraces. Having three or four bedrooms, terraced or, less frequently, semi-detached, often with a small back garden, rather than a shared back-yard, and equally often with some small walled area separating the front-door from the pavement, housing of this kind, although lacking some of the range of amenities to be found in the best of new housing, is popular and sought after. Indeed many of our respondents wanted to move into houses of precisely this kind, only to be disappointed.

Another one in ten of our households were also housed in fairly central areas, but in post-war, even new, council dwellings. There had been some (smaller) redevelopment schemes which pre-dated the St. Ann's programme as well as some modest new developments on land that had been reclaimed for housing from industrial use, and on patches of formerly open or waste-land. One such development in particular, on the edge of Radford, was completed just as the rehousing from the earlier phases of St. Ann's got underway, and a large number of these new houses and maisonettes were allocated to St. Ann's families. Most families were very happy with this arrangement, because it provided one element of continuity. Not all, however; one man we interviewed had very strongly-felt racial prejudices and had wanted to leave St. Ann's precisely because he resented the fact that it was a racially mixed community. To his acute distaste he found that his new neighbours were a West Indian family, rehoused from a nearby street in the old St. Ann's.

By far the largest group, and over 50% of our sample, had been rehoused on one of the very large council estates, some built before the Second World War, but most of post-war origin, which lie on the western perimeter of the City, from Bulwell in the North, to the giant and bleak Clifton Estate, constructed south of the River Trent in the early 1950s.

These estates vary greatly, one from another. For a start there is a well-understood hierarchy of esteem, or pecking-order, in which they are popularly held. At one end of this spectrum is an estate which was substantially completed before the war, which has a grimly monotonous and, for a stranger, confusing street-pattern of concentric circles, and is strikingly deficient in communal facilities of any kind. Few tenants actively choose to live on this estate; many of those allocated one of its houses try to arrange exchanges within the council sector, but find that the estate's general reputation travels before them, and experience a determined reluctance to co-operate on the part of fellow-exchangers.

At the other end of the spectrum are some of the other, more modern estates, which are visually more agreeable, are better maintained both inside and out, and are culturally and socially more stable, an impression reinforced by the neat and well-tended gardens, and the general air of quiet respectability.

For this reason it is hard to generalise about the perimeter estates. This much can be said, however. They are all very much more spacious than was either the old or is the new St. Ann's; the houses are bigger, are usually semi-detached and often have (by the more restricted standards of the 70s rather than those of the expansive 50s) very large front and back gardens. They all offer considerably more privacy than the congested streets and yards of old St. Ann's. Indeed, some people would argue that they offer so much privacy that the spontaneous generation of an involved public or communal life is all but impossible. The close (even too close) involvement of back-door gossip, and the vivid street life of St. Ann's, such folk will say, is replaced by imprisoning close-cropped privet-hedges, spring-shut front gates and dauntingly long front paths. In this environment a chance encounter or casual meeting may be quite unlikely, even with a next-door neighbour, while next door but one is barely within earshot.

1. *The Experience of Rehousing*

Bearing in mind people's somewhat strong apprehensions about moving, and the widespread confusion about the timing and the procedures associated with a move, and knowing as we now do, that our population was to be scattered to the four corners of the City, we were surprised to find that most households (72%) say that they were rehoused in the district that they wanted to live in. Only one household in four said they had accepted a house in a district or neighbourhood that was not of their first choice. Why these people had not been made an offer in their chosen area is not clear, although it is probable that the rhythm of demolition enforced some quick decisions. For all that, we are able to throw some light on why such people subsequently accepted an offer elsewhere in the City. Six respondents did so because, upon inspection, they liked the house and district that was offered to them. In a further two cases the house was near enough to their first-choice area to overcome any objection they might otherwise have had. The wishes of these eight households were not met in full, but the offer they received was close enough to their requirements to be acceptable to them. Three other households accepted a house in another district, thinking that this would be a temporary measure and that in due course they would be able to move again if they wished, presumably into the area of their first choice. In these cases, their present house, to begin with at least, was thought of as an interim or stopgap move, which represented an improvement on their house in St. Ann's, while falling short of their ultimate goal.

There remains another group, nearly twenty strong, who accepted the council's offer more grudgingly, or in response to strong social pressures. Five households did so in desperation. To live in an old house in a redevelopment area, to belong to a community that is being physically destroyed is, as we have shown, always painful; to some it becomes intolerable. Five of our respondents say that they moved because they could not bear to live in St. Ann's a day longer, and that this rejection was stronger than any reservations they may have had about the house and district that was being offered to them. To a family in this position, almost any alternative seems an improvement, and the will to insist upon an even greater, but hypothetical, improvement requires a strength of purpose that is hard to achieve and sustain.

As we pointed out in Chapter 2 the longer one waits for rehousing in a demolition zone, the more directly one feels the pressure to move. To dirt, is soon added bleakness, openness to the dusty winds; while, as the shops are evacuated or cleared, the initial advantages (so commonly claimed by our respondents in the earliest stages of our enquiry) are progressively eliminated. Shopping, far from being conveniently accessible, becomes a long uphill haul from distant outposts. One old lady whom we interviewed several times in our earlier enquiries suffered from chronic arthritis. She lived in a pitiful little house, raddled with damp, in a terrace at the top of a flight of mouldering stone stairs. As the neighbourhood crumbled around her, her condition showed drastic deterioration. We have not been able to find her since she has been resettled, but we are ready to believe that, towards the end of her ordeal, she would have happily moved to the North Pole if that was the only choice the Corporation could offer her.

Something of the same feeling of reluctant acceptance can be detected in the remaining group. These twelve households moved into another district from the one they wanted because they felt that they had little alternative. This does not, of course, mean that the Council adopted a "take-it or else" attitude, although the Council itself would be anxious that decisions to move were made speedily and without fuss. More likely, the tenant would discover, after looking at one or two houses, none in the district that he wanted most of all, that there was not a great deal to pick or choose between one house and another or between one estate and another. If, for whatever reason, there is no accommodation in the district that you really do want to live in, then any offer of a more or less similar house, in a more or less similar street becomes (less or more) equally acceptable.

Again, not everyone who accepted an offer of accommodation in some other than their favoured district, felt that they had made a bad decision. On the contrary, 60% of them thought that their new houses were better or much better than the old houses, and over a quarter thought that their new neighbourhood was an improvement on St. Ann's as a district to live in. Nevertheless, it is among this group of households that we find concentrated some of the most strongly felt grievances and strongly expressed complaints. The complaints cluster around three sets of circumstances. The most embittered and disgruntled group are those who were among the small group of owner-occupiers in the old St. Ann's. In most cases they never wished to move in the first place, they resent the fact that their houses were condemned and pulled down, and they resent the fact that they have now become tenants of rented property. It is perhaps misleading to say that they were not rehoused where they wished; in truth, they did not want to be rehoused at all, and might feel equally resentful wherever they were. A second and smaller group of complainants were some old-age pensioners, sometimes very old indeed, who never wished to move and dislike their new surroundings. In some cases this dislike stems from understandable problems of adjustment; we spoke to one old lady of 96 and another of 83 who each had lived in St. Ann's for more than 60 years and who were made very unhappy by the move. In the cases of some other old people, their unhappiness is more because they find their new houses inappropriate. Sometimes the house is too big for them, as they find it increasingly difficult to cope with daily household chores; sometimes their failing health creates an urgent need for single-storey, warden assisted housing.

Of course these are very genuine grievances, complaints moreover which may only have developed since the time of the removal, and which will very likely grow more acute as time passes. But it is important to note the very much larger group of old people who have reacted quite differently to their move, and who have been able to settle in happily and to thrive in their new homes.

There is one other group of people with strong complaints. They are not happy with their new houses for much the same reasons that they disliked their old ones. For example, there are those who are still cramped for space. These are normally the larger family units, with several young children, and they suffer because there is an acute shortage of larger houses with four or more bedrooms. Families of this sort simply have not experienced as great an improvement in their housing conditions as some others, and are consequently aggrieved. We should not forget that a physically smaller house in the old St. Ann's might easily have been partitioned into a larger number of rooms, so that four-bedroomed houses were not uncommon there. In the 1880s a developer could put two bedrooms up a rickety stair under the roof, and make three stories where later builders might blench to place two. In terms of family convenience, choice and privacy, therefore, a more solid house may be less acceptable.

Finally there are a handful of households who have unusual and exceptional housing requirements, which, they feel, have not been met. The ownership of pets was often the source of difficulty here. There was the man who bred rabbits in quantity and with regularity, or the lady with 12 cats, 2 dogs, several cage-birds and an impressive aquarium. There was the fishing enthusiast who bred his own maggots on a piece of rotting meat, who felt the neighbours revealed neither understanding nor tolerance. There were the pigeon-fanciers who found it difficult to come to grips with a new environment, consisting, they seemed to think, largely of restrictive bye-laws. Cases of this sort tax the ingenuity of even the most imaginative housing-manager.

In any event, our major finding is that most people said that they now live in the district they wanted. A close examination of people's expressed wishes in 1967/68, however, suggests an important qualification that should be made. Many people, perhaps most, did not have any very strongly expressed views on where they wanted to go. On the contrary many revealed some indifference about the alternative districts or estates. If people had strong views they were more likely to be about the size and type of house required and the list of household amenities considered essential than about any particular district of Nottingham. Naturally as the day when decisions are required draws closer, so it may be that people form stronger opinions, their wishes find a more concrete expression, they discover more about the alternatives open to them, they hear about other people's experiences and their reactions and so they develop clear-cut and specific wishes. No doubt this is sometimes the case; but it is our impression that many people remained open-minded to the very end. They waited to see what they were offered; they went to have a look; if they liked what they saw they took it, and in answer to our subsequent question they say, "Yes, this was the district we wanted to live in". But often comparison of their successive answers to questions asked at different times revealed that the desire to live in that district followed rather than preceded the decision to go there.

2. *The New House*

How do people like their new houses? We asked our respondents for a series of judgements comparing their present house with the old one they had occupied in St. Ann's, and we are now able to present a detailed appraisal of these reactions. The first set of questions which were entirely specific, elicited a very clear consensus: the great majority of people are highly appreciative of their new houses which they rate very much better than those they left behind. This finding is emphasised in no less than four separate queries each of which focused upon one structural aspect or another of the new houses.

Table IV:1
"How does this house compare with the house you lived in on .... Street in St. Ann's?"

	Very much better	Better	The same	Worse	Very much worse	n/a
General Assessment	47	34	8	7	1	2
Standard of Repair	33	39	18	5	3	2
Standard of Neighbourhood amenities	49	38	6	4	1	1
Number or size of rooms	19	52	14	11	3	1

We must bear in mind, however, that these questions clearly referred only to the physical structure and characteristics of the houses, and comparison was invited between them and the old decaying St. Ann's properties. It is therefore hardly surprising to find that nearly three quarters of our sample give the opinion that their new houses are in a better or very much better standard of repair than their old ones, since by any objective standard they *are* very much better. When one recalls that most of the St. Ann's houses lacked bathrooms and hot-water systems and had inconvenient and often semi-derelict lavatories, then one might readily expect to find that nearly nine people out of ten think (as nine out of ten of our sample did think), that a newer, usually post-war, house with indoor lavatory and bathroom, and a hot-water system in both bathroom and kitchen represents a great improvement in household amenities. Who can doubt it? A convincing seven out of ten also think that the rooms themselves are superior. They are normally larger, drier, easier to heat, often supplied with power points, certainly endowed with windows and doors that fit, and that usually open and shut normally. Small wonder, then, that over 80% of our respondents, when asked for a general assessment of their new house, rate it as better or very much better. Small wonder perhaps, but a finding that nonetheless deserves close attention because it reflects a real and important achievement in housing standards which is clearly felt, understood for what it is and appreciated. The City Housing Department which is so often the target of serious and sustained criticism, may perhaps take some comfort from these figures which indicate unmistakeable and overwhelming approval by the population most directly affected, of an authentic transformation of their physical environment. That said and emphasised, it must not be forgotten that there remains a large proportion of our original population about whose fate we know little or nothing, but who may well be in considerably less eligible circumstances. We must also consider the views of the small group (usually fewer than 1 in 10) who are very unhappy with their new houses, and, as we shall see when we move from questions of the physical environment to those referring to the social environment, the picture of general well-being and contentment requires substantial modification.

Turning to the small sample of 12 households who expressed some general dissatisfaction with their new house, we find in at least seven cases that the houses they now occupy represent no improvement at all, and in five cases are actually worse. These families were among the small group of households who were originally living in some of the very best houses in the old St. Ann's. Although St. Ann's was composed in the main of terraced housing, there were a few streets which were altogether more substantial semi-detached or detached properties. Cutting across part of the old St. Ann's, and in great contrast to its surroundings, was a tree-lined pedestrian way called Robin Hood Chase, along which were built large Victorian detached and semi-detached villas with generous gardens. From the right vantage point, and looking in the right direction, down the Chase, it was possible, although in the heart of St. Ann's to obtain a bizarre and quite uncharacteristic impression of rustic charm. From the same vantage point, and looking in the other direction, one stared straight into the surrounding reality of the slum. When first built, the houses on Robin Hood Chase were certainly occupied by the more prosperous tradesmen and professional people. By the mid-sixties, some of these houses had become multi-occupied tenements and were in as deplorable state of repair as the nearby terraces. Others remained in good condition and were still family houses, still occupied by the more prosperous tradesman and the odd professional person.

Four of our twelve dissatisfied families had been moved from larger homes of this sort, two actually from Robin Hood Chase itself. Generally, these people had exchanged a large and spacious house for a smaller one. Sometimes the smaller house was simpler to run, cheaper to heat and easier to clean or had some other advantage. But this was outweighed by the sense that the older house had a spaciousness, a character, even an elegance that no standard council house could replace. One particular example can illustrate the point. We spoke to an elderly couple, now retired, who had lived for over 15 years on Robin Hood Chase. In 1968 they had made some minor complaints about the house; the roof was causing a problem with damp. But by and large they liked living in a house with five bedrooms and three receptions rooms, to say nothing of a spacious garden. Moreover they had a high regard for St. Ann's as a district; it was conveniently close to town, but there were also good shopping facilities near at hand. People were friendly and kind, and although there were a few vandals and hooligans who caused trouble, most people were sociable and neighbourly. Not unnaturally this couple were not eager to move; there are benefits to be derived from living in a close-knit neighbourhood, and if one is effectively sheltered from the crucial disadvantage of deplorable housing conditions then these benefits can be appreciated without serious qualification.

This couple now live in a little modern house on an estate on the northern edge of the City. In fact they have settled in very well, and have few complaints to make about their present house or the neighbourhood. They find their new neighbours friendly, when they have the time to be friendly. Moreover they could see that redevelopment would make a real improvement to the housing circumstances of many of their old neighbours. Nonetheless they retained the warmest memories of their old house which they described as "spacious and beautiful". They produced an album of photographs of Robin Hood Chase, with its large houses, its trees and grass verges, and one could easily understand their nostalgia. But at the same time one remembered that they were among the lucky handful whose housing conditions in old St. Ann's were so markedly above average.

There were four families who had moved from larger to smaller properties in this way. Each of them had similarly kind recollections of the old St. Anns, and each of them disliked what they had seen of the new St. Ann's. Curiously they each expressed this dislike in identical terms, referring to the uniformity of the new houses. The new St. Ann's, said one old lady, who now lived in a block designed for old people, had the atmosphere of a prison-camp; to a middle-aged couple who had been owner-occupiers of a large house on Bluebell Hill Road, the new St. Ann's was "like an army barracks"; another couple, who with their three brothers had lived in a seven-roomed home on Hungerhill Road, would not move back into the new St. Ann's because "it's like an army-camp". These reactions we report as we received them: we do not suggest that others would necessarily agree with them.

The other major source of dissatisfaction with their new housing was expressed by people who felt that it was inappropriate to their special needs. Here we encounter people whose personal circumstances, usually ill-health, old age or a combination of both, prevent them from liking their new houses. We cited earlier a lady of 96 who feels isolated and alone in her new pensioners' flat; she realises that her extreme age and failing health are major causes of her difficulties, and acknowledges that for many younger people, the new housing may be much better. But she feels uprooted, cut off from the old friends and neighbours whom she remembers on Moffatt Street. Two elderly sisters who moved from Pym Street made the same point; they don't know anyone now, and miss the old back-yard meetings and chats. But they too are conscious that, for many, redevelopment has brought improvements; as one put it, "it's been a damned good clearance out of the old houses", and even while remembering the sociability of the back-yard, they also remember, towards the end, being frightened to go out into the yard because of the rats. Then there is the middle-aged man whose health has failed and is now an invalid. He lives in an agreeable house, but is unable to climb the stairs and so lives in one downstairs room. What he really wants is a bungalow, as he is quite unable to enjoy his new house properly. Moreover he has lost the network of social contacts he maintained in his old house on Beverley Street, which he thinks might well have made his life easier than he finds it now, among strangers, on the Aspley side of town.

3. Shops, Work and Schools

We then asked our respondents to compare their present house with their old one, with respect to the convenience of access to shops, to work, and to schools. A study of their replies, however, shows that they may go far beyond questions of simple convenience to form a more comprehensive set of judgements concerned with quality of service as much as access to it.

Table IV:2 summarises their answers;

Table IV:2

"How does your present house compare for access with you lived in on . . . . Street in St. Ann's?"

	Very much better	Better	Same	Worse	Very much worse	n/a
Shops	2	8	36	36	13	5
*Work	3	10	54	29	4	
*Schools	9	29	52	9	1	

*Families without children could not comment on schools, and those where no one was at work could not comment on the convenience to the work-place. The don't-know and no answer categories have therefore been deleted and the percentage refers to the distribution of those who did have an answer to the question.

It is at once clear that the generally high level of satisfaction with the house itself, does not extend quite so generally, nor at so high a level, to these three basic characteristics of the neighbourhood. On the contrary, we see that exactly half of our sample find that the shopping facilities upon which they now depend are actually worse or much worse than they used to be in St. Ann's, and only one household in ten thinks that shopping facilities have improved. The wide variety of shops in the old St. Ann's, with its extended network of little "beer-offs", or its two major high streets accommodating larger stores, multiples and specialist tradesmen, and its proximity to the central market and the large department stores of Central Nottingham, was, as we have noted, one of the few significantly advantageous features of the old district. Moreover, thanks in part to the vigorous public defence of their own interest mounted by small shopkeepers threatened by redevelopment, this amenity value was acknowledged from the start. In our earlier surveys we asked the residents of St. Ann's what characteristics of the old district they thought they would miss when it was pulled down, and the feature that was mentioned more than any other was the shops. In the event, however, when asked in 1976 to comment on the things that they have come to miss about the old St. Ann's, "friends and neighbours" are the lack which is mentioned most often. Even so, 30% of our respondents still say that they miss the shops, and one can readily see why. In most cases the variety and choice of shops, the wide range of commodities on offer at prices to suit most, if not all, pockets, has been replaced by a greatly restricted access to fewer shops, unstimulated by commercial competition, less immediately responsive to local consumer demand, and often considerably further away. In the old St. Ann's, if one had the money, the time and the enthusiasm for it, one could indulge a form of hunting instinct as one prowled along St. Ann's Well Road or Alfred Street from butcher to butcher, greengrocer to greengrocer, and second-hand store to junk-shop. Nowadays shopping in St. Ann's is as bland and dull an exercise as on the other estates, with the one small supermarket, the single newsagent and tobacconist, the solitary monopolist butcher. In St. Ann's itself, in the main shopping precinct (deathly phrase) there is one smallish general store which rather desperately, but very unconvincingly, tries to evoke the atmosphere and the spirit of the lost corner-shops.

A severe reduction in the number and variety of shops may well make sound economic sense to the businessmen who secure the available franchises. At one level it might make a kind of economic sense to the customer, if it were to be shown convincingly that such concentration of enterprise, combined with economies of scale, serves to reduce prices below the levels prevailing in the corner-shops. But there is more to a market than simple commerce; it satisfies other instincts than primary needs, so that a transaction may be a trophy for one party, and a profit for the other. But a market, or a busy shopping street, is also a public place, a forum, a locus where friends meet and strangers mingle with an unspoken common purpose.

Reading through the comments about the shops the same ones recur again and again. Fewer shops; no choice between one store and another; no wide selection of goods within; only the basic shopping requirements catered for at the nearest shops; the old gossipy atmosphere has gone, no one has time to pause for a chat anymore; much further to walk and to carry bags than before; the shops are only open during conventional shopping hours; they don't have the same feeling about them.

These reactions register, from the consumer end of the spectrum, a series of disadvantages which have been borne in upon planners and public policy-makers with increasing force. In Nottingham, not only have the long cross-roads of Alfred Street and St. Ann's Well Road been ground under the dozers and demolition gear: so too, in the Meadows district, have the mile of shops along Arkwright Street, which led from the Station to Trent Bridge, past a dozen little restaurants, several pubs, two fishing tackle shops, a jazz-record collectors' paradise, a little stamp-shop, umpteen antique vendors, and a variety of watchmakers, cobblers, and other artisan tradesmen. After these clearances, a question-mark hangs over Alfreton Road and Radford. There grows a positive dearth of sites in which specialist interests can be met, or low-overhead trades carried on. It is perhaps a happy chance that the fashion for long hair continues to prevail among younger men: if it did not, there are now nothing like the necessary numbers of establishments which could house the numbers of barbers who have been evicted during slum-clearance. The rents, and the rates, of little bits of the great new trading monoliths into which markets are being concentrated are quite prohibitive to the small traders upon whom whole communities have been accustomed to depend for a rich variety of facilities.

The attraction of the old Central Market, or of the present Sneinton Market, the magnet that draws a throng every Saturday to the Cattle Market, involves the search for a bargain, but is more than that; it includes, for some, a grim economic necessity, but for others it is the exercise of a freedom. It is both a commercial expression, and an assertion of citizenship, of membership of a community. Shopping can be both a necessary chore and a sociable activity and, to the extent that this is true, the restriction of choice to the single, sanitised, pre-packed, muzack world of a supermarket chain-store is in nobody's best interest.

4. The New District: General Reactions

Further widening the scope of our investigation, we next asked a series of questions about the new neighbourhoods in which our respondents found themselves. Some questions were concerned with straightforward reactions and opinions, while in others we asked for comparisons to be made between the new districts and the old St. Ann's.

We started with a very general query asking

people what they thought of their new district as a place to live in. Table I shows the distribution of answers, column I for their new district, and column II the answer to the identical question posed when they were still living in St. Ann's eight years earlier.

Table IV:3
"What do you think of the district as a place to live?"

	1976 %	1967/68 %
Very satisfied	25	11
Satisfied	55	28
Neutral	10	16
Dissatisfied	6	19
Very dissatisfied	4	26

Eight households out of ten now express some degree of satisfaction, and only one out of ten any real dissatisfaction. This is a striking contrast to the response we received from the same people to the same question, posed when they were still in their old houses. On that occasion, over four times as many people expressed some dissatisfaction, a dissatisfaction which was felt strongly and intensely, whilst fewer than four families out of ten were willing to voice any satisfaction at all.

On the face of it, then, the general approval that was registered with respect to the new housing seems to extend to the district as a whole. However, closer examination of the evidence on housing has shown that the judgements that are being made are complex ones, with a more guarded approval of some particular aspects of the wider environment and a number of very trenchant criticisms being made even by those who are, in general, among the most approving. This suggests that the section of the survey dealing specifically with neighbourhood questions merits the same close scrutiny to see in detail what expressions of satisfaction are referring to, and what underlying reservations are being made. Indeed, suspicions are immediately aroused by the answers to our next question, "How does this district compare with the old St. Ann's?"

Table IV:4
"How does this district compare with the old St. Ann's?"

	%
Very much better	21
Better	36
About the same	20
Worse	18
Very much worse	5

Here we see that although rather more than half of our respondents thought their new districts better or very much better than the old St. Ann's, nearly a quarter thought it worse or very much worse. And to confuse the matter still further over a third of those who thought their new district worse than the old St. Ann's nonetheless were generally satisfied or in some cases very satisfied with their new areas!

It is clear that some very finely balanced judgements are being made, subtle and ingenious assessments which shrewdly weigh the variety of advantages and disadvantages on a number of widely different kinds of scale at once.

It would make our task much easier if opinions were divided neatly and consistently between those who liked the changes on the one hand, and those who don't on the other. But in most cases, people both like and dislike, approve and disapprove, are enthusiastic about some things and have reservations about others. Although there are certain patterns which emerge quite clearly from our material, we were never allowed to forget that our sample comprised 141 households, each one of which was unique and distinct. It is not easy to make some coherent sense of the material we have gathered, without losing the texture of the different responses we heard.

There are certain basic observations that can be made without difficulty. The feature of the new neighbourhoods which commands the widest approval is better housing, following by the feeling that the new environment is healthier, cleaner and quieter. In all three respects these judgements are accurate. By any objective standard of construction, amenity and repair the housing is better than most of the old houses that were knocked down. The space standards that have been applied both within the new houses and between houses, means that population densities have been greatly reduced, which alone would suggest that people will suffer less from noise generated by their neighbours. The increasing segregation of residential from industrial premises, characteristic of housing and planning policy throughout the post-war period has reduced the nuisance of industrial noise, dirt, atmospheric and other pollution. Similarly it has dispersed the concentration of noisy, smelly and dangerous traffic generated by industrial deliveries, which was one of the most distressing features of the old St. Ann's. We have documented some of this already, in the prolonged story of the pie factory and Plantagenet Street.

These three improvements are re-emphasised in the answers to our question "Is there anything about the old St. Ann's that you are glad to be rid of?" Here, the general disrepair of the houses and the increasing dereliction of the neighbourhood are mentioned most often, followed by the constant high noise-levels and the problem of vermin, particularly rats.

On the negative side, the features of the new districts which attract the greatest criticism are first, complaints about other people, problems of unfriendly neighbours, of friction, and of suspicion. This is followed by complaints about the range of relative inconveniences associated with estate life, some of which we have already discussed. The inconveniences most often mentioned relate specifically to the built-in advantages of the old St. Ann's: its shops and its closeness to town.

In short, we begin to see emerging the same cluster of good points and bad that become clear from the earlier evidence about housing conditions. The great advantage of newer and larger houses in an altogether more spacious and less congested environment, with everything that this implies for the quality of personal and home life has been seized on. For many of our respondents this still represents, after several years, an important, for some an intoxicating, change for the better in their daily circumstances. It means liberation from the cycle of thankless household drudgery, the endless rearguard action against damp, dirt and decay, to the incomparably more comfortable routine of normal family chores, which yield tangible results.

However, as soon as one opens the front-door and leaves the privacy of the family home, anxieties and complaints start to gather force. The practical problems are in fact part and parcel of lower population densities; fewer shops at a greater distance; fewer immediately local work-opportunities, particularly for part-time and women workers; less frequent bus-services; inconveniences of time and distance, and finally, beyond the immediately practical problems, the more intangible, but no less real, anxieties about lost friends, familiar neighbours of long standing, the network of social contacts that prolonged residence anywhere permits but that slum-environments seem to encourage particularly vigorously.

V Family, Neighbourhood and Community

"Perceptions of housing problems tend also to be biased in favour of physical rather than social manifestations. Any review of the literature on housing, particularly official surveys of conditions in the census and by central departments, will show that disproportionate attention is given to physical appearance, amenities and layout compared with social and economic allocation and use and financial cost . . . visual eyesores are easier than the special social and financial problems that certain kinds of family have in restrictive physical settings to communicate to councillors, officials and the public. They dominate the preoccupations, training and organisation, for example, of the architectural and planning professions." Peter Townsend: *Poverty in the United Kingdom,* 1979, p.479.

1. *New Districts and Old: Family Life.*

This vital question, the impact of physical reconstruction on the social fabric of a neighbourhood, is one that recurs so frequently and insistently in the housing literature that we were determined from the outset to examine it in some detail. At the time of the first survey we had been struck by the complexity and ambiguity of family and neighbourhood relationships. It seemed likely that the impact of redevelopment could only be to add fresh complications.

One of the most persistent criticisms to be levelled at local authority housing policies, and particularly at policies involving major redevelopment, is that they damage long-established kinship networks. Attention is regularly drawn to the very considerable extent to which the daily life of working-class communities remains rooted in extended family ties, expressed not just as sentimental attachments, but in a host of regular exchanges of services, mutually recognised rights and obligations that help people to sustain their normal patterns of life. The key relationship, we are often told, is that between a mother and her married daughters, which persists across the generations to provide some continuity of experience and expectation amounting to a significant cultural pattern.

Housing policy, and particularly redevelopment, to the extent that it physically separates members of a family one from another, is thought to undermine these kinship ties, isolating people into smaller nuclear family groups, causing inconvenient disruption to the lives of working mothers, who can no longer share the burden of child-rearing with a helpful granma, and bringing loneliness and frustration to the aged. From Young and Willmott onwards, this theme has been reported so frequently that it is widely accepted as a generally valid statement, even a truism, that redevelopment undermines family ties.

To an outsider, the old St. Ann's appeared to be precisely the sort of district in which one would expect to find this traditional network of extended family ties, where complex patterns of self-help and mutual aid would normally go some way to enable hard-pressed residents to cope with the problems of daily life in a slum. In fact, however, our study of 1968 revealed what seemed to us at the time to be a relatively weak kinship system. For example, fewer people seemed to be involved in regular family ties than was the case on a long-established council estate elsewhere in Nottingham that we examined in 1968, or in many other studies undertaken in the '50s and '60s on family life in working-class districts. More precisely, little more than half (56%) of those of our 1968 respondents whom we were later able to reinterview had had relatives living in St. Ann's or nearby, with whom they maintained any significant contact, compared with over 70% of those who were living on the council estate, at the same time. Consequently, nearly a half of our sample had no opportunity, even if they wished it, to develop the habits of family mutual aid that were so central an ingredient of social life in parts of the East End of London and elsewhere. Instead they had to rely more upon their own resources, or upon assistance from friends and neighbours. Beyond doubt there was a great deal of such assistance and mutual aid, although here again as the pace of redevelopment quickened, and the need for help and support intensified under the strain, so the possibilities narrowed. One by one families were removed, inadvertently leaving their erstwhile neighbours in greater physical and social isolation.

Even in a weakened state, family ties remained an important part of the social fabric and one in which we necessarily retained an interest. Had we been able to foresee our 1976 findings we may well have taken a more prolonged and probing interest earlier, for we discovered that, among the 1976 rehoused sample there are now many more, rather than fewer, family contacts that there had been in the wider sample we spoke with ten years before. The proportion of respondents who now said they had members of their family living nearby has risen from 56% to 82%. 29% of our 1976 sample, who had no family nearby before, now say that they do have some relatives with whom they maintain some significant, and in a goodly number of cases regular, contact. This is an interesting and unexpected finding, which requires some further discussion.

The actual numbers of families maintaining regular contact now amounted to something under half the total, as will be seen from Table V:1.

Table V:1
Frequency of Family Contact

Do you still see your family	No.	%
Regularly?	66	47
Occasionally?	40	28
Seldom	11	8
Never?	1	1
N/a	23	16

Of these households taken together, 48 said they

were further away from their nearest relatives since redevelopment, while 68 were nearer to them or "about the same". Cutting across these responses, 89 people thought their move had made no difference to the possibility of family contact: these 89, naturally include some who never had any such contact anyway, and some who had no live relatives anywhere, as well as those people who have experienced no undue difficulty in sustaining existing links.

Of course, it must be stressed that there is a difference between the original samples upon whose testimony our previously published reports rested, and our current "1968" sample which consists only of those people with whom we were able to resume contact in 1976. Those original respondents missing from the later survey have, for the purposes of this argument, been excluded from the comparative data from the earlier investigation. This arbitrary decision does not affect many of the judgements we present in this report, but it does affect our assessment on this particular matter. Those who refer to our earlier writings will find that the extended family was far less prevalent in the old St. Ann's that it is, apparently, among rehoused St. Ann's residents. Part of the reason for this is that the old St. Ann's had a remarkably rapid turnover of population in some streets, notably in those owned by the Corporation, where the houses were utilised systematically for the housing of so-called "problem" families. Another part of it is that the old St. Ann's housed a variety of stable immigrant populations in accommodation which was often owner-occupied, and some of these communities seem to have rehoused themselves in different districts, also in properties which are generally owner-occupied.

Numbers of Italian migrants seem to have moved to the Sneinton area, for instance. Wherever national or ethnic groups have fallen out of the Corporation's area of responsibility, they have also fallen out of our enquiry, since the Council's housing records do not enable us to trace them. Yet, clearly, many immigrant families will remain "nuclear" units until the time their children reach the age of marriage and autonomy, at which point we must expect new extended family units to emerge. All this is a function of the age-structure of the various immigrant communities, which of course varies with the time of their arrival, since in general, migrants have tended to some extent to cluster not only by place of origin, but also to some degree by age-group. Tantalisingly, we do not have hard evidence on such matters, except in those rare cases in which migrants have been allocated council houses.

None of these necessary caveats minimise the importance of the findings of this enquiry. What it shows is that adequate rehousing may move some way towards reversing the adverse pressure of the declining slum on the institutions of extended family. Before redevelopment young marrieds commonly fled the old St. Ann's if they possibly could, and then found continued regular family contact within the old district more difficult. It now seems that married children are somewhat more, rather than less, likely to be able to maintain their parental links after redevelopment than they were before it.

Among our 1968 sample were 39 families (27% of all the families interviewed) with growing children, then in their teens, who, by 1976, were grown-up and who had in a number of cases, particularly if they had married, left home to set up their own independent households. Thus a substantial group of parents had no relatives "nearby" in 1968 (because they were all still members of the original nuclear family) but are now involved in the extended-family relationship with their adult children, extending to other newly-formed households.

But there is another reason why there may be more family contacts now, after rehousing, than before. This is that the presence of relatives in another part of the city may itself have encouraged a tenant to elect to be rehoused in that particular area. The residents of St. Ann's were asked to indicate whereabouts they would like to be rehoused; such preferences inevitably involve questions of the type of housing people prefer, prevailing levels of rent, and so forth. There is no doubt, though, that the whereabouts of friends and relations must always weigh heavily in the making of such choices. Of course, the local authority was not able in all cases to meet people's wishes fully, but in many they were clearly able to offer accommodation which was nearer than the old St. Ann's home to other family members. Thus, of that group of extended families which was involved in regular contacts both in 1968 and again in 1976, 52% were rehoused either nearer to their relatives or at least no further away, whereas 71% of those households who have now for the first time reported regular visitations with their relatives were in this situation. This clearly suggests a relationship between closeness and contact, even when one allows for the maturing of children and their establishment of new households.

Even where people were rehoused away from their relatives, the fact that the Corporation was universal landlord opened up a considerable possibility of re-adjustment. Whilst exchanges of council houses remain possible, there remains an important access or safeguard for the maintenance of extended family ties. Of course, widespread sales of council houses might well inhibit this fluid (and for us, desirable) state of affairs. Once the stock of houses available for exchange is restricted past a certain point, mobility will become a much more sluggish and difficult operation.

Both these possible reasons for increased family contacts are simple, obvious even, but their importance is not for that reason to be denied. But there is a third possible reason which, if true, would also be important. This explanation is difficult to measure with any accuracy, because it has to be deduced from odd remarks that people make, from throwaway (but revealing) comments, from carefully reading between the lines of an interview. Put at its simplest, some households have renewed contact with other members of their families in different households because only now, rehoused, do they feel able to do so.

There are at least two dimensions to this new ability. First, there is a purely physical enablement. Rehoused families from St. Ann's have in most cases moved to houses which are larger than the houses they left behind, large enough, and sufficiently provided with basic amenities, to enable people to enjoy more comfortable conditions and social possibilities, and to share this enjoyment with their friends and relatives. Secondly, and perhaps more important, some people may now feel more able to acknowledge their families psychologically and morally. The move to superior accommodation can lift from some people a sense of humiliation, even of failure or stigma, which was sometimes associated with living in slum housing. Where this existed, it could have inhibited relationships between members of a family, different sections of which were experiencing considerable differences in housing conditions. This is probably most true within each generation, rather than across generations. Siblings, cousins, (and similarly age-related family connections) may well share broadly similar social and material expectations (and consequently experience satisfaction or disappointment as the case may be) that are different from the judgements and responses made about what is appropriate as between one generation and another. Here, perhaps, we can get a glimpse of the way in which differential changes in material standards of living have impacted upon family life. In *Family and Kinship and East London* we get an image of family life which is culturally homogeneous and in which most people have grown up in an environment of relative material hardship. This has emphasised the need for mutual aid within the family. Those who were rehoused in Greenleigh, in superior accommodation, were exceptional, and felt most strongly their breach with the old social ties. But what may have been true of Bethnal Green in the early '50s, is not necessarily true of St. Ann's (or even of Bethnal Green) a generation later. First, council-housing as a proportion of the housing stock has increased from 18% in 1951 to 32% in 1978. This proportion is of course much higher among working-class families who have not been able to maintain their share in the expansion of owner-occupation. Nowadays council-housing, mostly purpose built over the last 50 years, is the predominant form of working-class housing. Secondly, the general rise in living standards since the Second World War has been reflected in a considerably greater social emphasis being put on the possession of consumer goods, including a range of durable household goods. Although it can be overstressed, there is little doubt that to some extent, a family sense of identity and achievement has become reflected in the possession of such goods, as an indication of material success. The possession of these goods depends first of all upon a sufficient command over resources to afford the price, or more normally, the credit to make the purchase. But it also depends upon having a living-space which is large enough to install the goods and equipped (with power points or plumbing) to enable them to be used. In the old St. Ann's the rooms were too small to hold much furniture (although one was constantly amazed to discover how much can be crammed into a small space given sufficient determination), and in many cases too damp for its long life. The constrictions upon material acquisitions were most marked in the kitchen. Not only were the kitchens in the old St. Ann's too small to hold much more than a cooker, but they were certainly not wired to allow tenants to put in fridges, freezers, washing machines, spin-dryers, electric kettles, toasters, irons, and all the other electrically-powered gadgets, useful or otherwise, that a well-equipped kitchen is supposed to marshall. Usually they possessed a light, and that would be all. Sometimes even the light was missing.

We shall examine these matters further in Chapter VI: what is clear is that this kind of constriction was, throughout the '60s, increasingly felt as a deprivation. From some of those who were still close to their relatives in 1968, we heard remarks about how grubby they felt when they compared their housing and hence household situation and domestic possibilities with the housing conditions enjoyed by other members of the family.

This feeling was not simply a matter of "keeping up with the Jones". It was poignantly expressed in a television feature which we helped to prepare for the Thames channel, in which one young family explained the disabilities of slum housing by direct comparison with the condition of their siblings on a Council Estate. Every time you papered a wall in the slum, it would be raddled with damp within weeks. New furniture deteriorated rapidly. To maintain even the appearance of cleanliness was a daily and inexorable drudge. Yet on the estate, where the fabric of the buildings was adequate to modern living standards, once a job of decoration had been done, it would be expected to last, and wear and tear upon the furnishings was restricted to the normal hazards of family use. The old houses were a constant drain on money, effort and time, and they certainly produced, in some people, a tendency to withdraw from close contact with contrasting experiences. So striking was the description of this condition by the family in the TV documentary that they were inundated with offers of help, and we still meet people who remember exactly what was said in that short clip of film. Without putting too much weight on this dimension of the problem, we remain convinced that it should be seriously considered.

2. Friends and Neighbours

Families may be one thing. Neighbours, we are often told, are another. And of nowhere was this more true than in St. Ann's. On the one hand we came across many examples of long-standing relationships between neighbours and friends, with highly developed systems of mutual aid and dependency. On the other hand, we came across many who felt socially isolated, knew very few people and relied upon no one but themselves. At the level of local gossip we eavesdropped on conversations about third parties that were inquisitive, meddling, even salty, but were also good-humoured, tolerant and fundamentally kindly. But we sometimes overheard remarks and rumours about others which were aggressive, even violent. Community can have two faces: intolerant and uncaring, as well as supporting, vindictive and mean-spirited as well as kindly and generous. We quickly came to understand that the relationships generated in the backyard, on the doorstep, or at the street-corner were not always helpful or harmonious, and that some well-known and acclaimed accounts, while expressing an important part of the truth, have overlooked or omitted many of the cross-tensions that we found everywhere we looked. Our first surveys in the late '60s strengthened these feelings when we examined the answers to the question "On this street is it better to get on well with the neighbours or is it better to keep yourself to yourself". 54% of our respondents said they tried to get on well with their neighbours, while 42% said they kept themselves to themselves and 4% didn't know. These figures seem to catch very well this ambiguity.

After people had been rehoused they were somewhat less ambivalent. 61% (an increase of 7%) now say that they prefer to "get on well", whilst there has been a decline in the numbers wishing to keep themselves apart. The "don't knows" have almost disappeared. Even these changed responses still reflect the mix of wanting to get on well, but with reservations about the wisdom of involving oneself too closely with other people, and still reveal the tension between a natural friendliness and a wariness particularly towards newcomers or strangers.

Yet in our later enquiry, we were able to sharpen our focus on this indeterminate issue. When we asked "is this a friendly street to live on?" nearly 8 out of 10 people said that it was, and only one-fifth did not find it so. This would appear to reveal a high degree of apparent friendliness. Certainly, it does not suggest that our rehoused population as a whole felt itself isolated, cut off from social contacts, or yet surrounded by hostility (or even indifference). Yet strangely, as people have moved into what our enquiry shows, by comparison with their earlier responses, to have been a more hospitable environment, nonetheless their own recollections seem to have warmed up, retrospectively, the memories of the old St. Ann's. When asked "is this street as friendly as the one you lived on before?" only 30% thought that it was, while over 50% were sure that it was not. One-fifth of the people could not detect any noticeable difference. Is it possible that this apparent warmth towards yesterday reflects the greater ease and informality of life in the close-knit, not to say crowded, environment of St. Ann's? Could it be that, friendly though most agree the council estates to be, they are part of a more formally regulated and ordered social existence? Or might it flow simply from nostalgia, in which the kindnesses of slum life are remembered, while its animosities are mercifully put behind?

That this may be (at least in part) the case is suggested by the answers we received to two other questions we put in our surveys of 1967 and 1968. We asked respondents who were facing redevelopment what, if anything, they thought that they would miss from the old St. Ann's, and what they would gladly be rid of. Some of their answers to these questions have already been discussed but it is important to stress that a quarter of our respondents thought that they would miss their neighbours, while about one in eight wanted to be rid of theirs (we have no means of establishing in how many cases, if any, each group was referring specifically to the other!).

In 1976, when we asked the same population what they now missed, and what they were glad to be rid of, we find a different but neatly symmetrical set of answers. The number of families who, whatever they said in 1967/68, now say that they do in the event miss their old neighbours has increased by over half to 38% of the total. The number who say that they are glad to be shot of their old neighbours has dropped by half, to 7%. Indeed of all the things that people now miss, the neighbours are easily the most often cited. Only the shops, mentioned in 30% of our cases, comes anywhere near to them. There are two other parts to these questions that add something to this discussion. When asked in 1967/68 what they thought that they would miss, our respondents gave us fairly concrete and specific answers such as their friends, the corner-shop, nearness to town, etc. Only 1 respondent made particular reference to the pubs of old St. Ann's, one of the great unsung social amenities of that district, while 5% of them talked, necessarily vaguely, about the special atmosphere they detected in St. Ann's, the particular character that made it different from other areas, even other deprived areas.

But looking back in 1976, 8% now find that they miss their old pubs, even among those who have settled in with every evident sign of well-being and comfort in a public-bar in their new locality. Meanwhile, the 5% who sensed the special atmosphere of St. Ann's has now grown to 15% who, unprompted, indicate that this feeling about a familiar district is missed. Atmosphere is a vague notion, but taken in conjunction with the other points that were being stressed, it clearly refers to the quite unstructured and casual ways in which people were constantly thrown together, contacts that were encouraged by the physical lay-out and design of the old area, but which, in the view of some of our families, are actively discouraged and inhibited by the lay-out and design of modern housing-estates. Many of our older respondents made this point to us with great emphasis. It is of course the pensioners and those who have retired, who have the most free time to spend in casual socialising. They do not have the same pressing and time-consuming commitments as families with young children, and they have the greatest need of such informal contacts if they are not to live in considerable loneliness and isolation. So it was particularly from our elderly respondents that we heard this complaint time and again. And several of these elderly people have a very clear grasp of why they felt isolated even from their nearest neighbours. For a start it was not simply that people were inclined to be less friendly than formerly. True, they may well be preoccupied with their own affairs, and sometimes there may be a certain reserve or reticence in the face of newcomers and strangers. Occasionally, we came across allegations of prejudice, of stigma, of active hostility, but this was quite exceptional. In general there was believed to be a basic willingness on the part of most people to be agreeable, and to be helpful when necessary. But the design of a modern estate makes it very difficult for this willingness to be demonstrated spontaneously. One old lady living in an old person's flat in the new St. Ann's pointed out that, unlike the old terraced houses, her living-room window doesn't look out over the street or indeed any thoroughfare. In consequence she is literally unable to see, or be seen by, passers by. She repeated the by now familiar complaint that you no longer bump into people quite casually at the street corner or in the shop. This particular old soul, more gregarious than many, also misses the small local pub, and finds the new local too big, too impersonal and lacking the cosiness and simple intimacy of the old. In each case she draws attention to questions of planning and design decisions, which have overlooked the need for low-key, off-hand, unplanned meetings between people, without which informal neighbourly networks cannot readily develop.

Much the same point was made in many other interviews. There was a housewife, now on the Bestwood Estate, who said "People want to get on well with one another, but up here you don't see anyone from one week to the next. The way they built it all makes people strangers". Another family, now living in Wollaton, said "You never see anybody to talk to, everyone goes their own ways, no one pops in for a cup of tea anymore". Again and again, people used the same word to convey their differences to us. St. Ann's, they said, had been "cosy". And the cosiness they had in mind was a social phenomenon. In their new houses people are physically "cosier"; they are warmer and drier and considerably more comfortable. But they are more comfortable on their own, and they have lost the easy opportunity to have a chat about nothing in particular, to pop in, for no special reason. Of course people are not prevented from meeting one another on an estate, but it is made more difficult by front doors that are meant to be safely shut rather than scullery doors that were usually open. No one walks down a garden-path and knocks on a door without a good reason for doing so. As one housewife on Clifton estate told us, "In St. Ann's anyone would talk to you, but out here, I'd have to hang over the garden-gate to see anyone, and they still wouldn't talk — they'd think I was barmy!" Social contacts on an estate become more fundamental, more purposeful, more instrumental, but in the process they lose their 'cosiness', their spontaneity and intimacy.

They may also become more threatening. Several of our families told us that they were now actively discouraging closer contacts with their new neighbours because it only brings problems. For some families, living in the cocoon of their own private home, the neighbours, living in their own adjacent cocoon, only impinged when they wanted something. One man told us "It doesn't do to be too friendly, you only get put upon".

There is a constant tension between people's desire for some privacy, to get on with their lives as they think best, and their wish for fruitful social contacts. In our earlier enquiries we formed the view that the old St. Ann's permitted people to have too little privacy. The houses were too close to one another; there were too many thin party-walls; the communal backyards threw people together whether they liked it or not; front-doors that open directly onto the pavement make the pavement and its traffic an extension of the living room. The only space you could call your own was the small cramped rooms within your own house, and we found many families who guarded this private space with great jealousy. To be invited into a house to continue a chat that started on the doorstep or in the yard was a real privilege, because it was an invitation to share the only bit of private space that people had at their command. But the corollary of this was that there was a sense of communal ownership, or at the least, communal access, everywhere else in St. Ann's. The backyards were under the control of those who lived on them, but the streets and pavements belonged to everyone. Passers-by who strolled down the pavement were strolling past you, and were, for that instant, in some relationship with you, no matter how tenuous or short-lived.

On the estates, this feeling is almost entirely lost. Each house, or block of houses, is surrounded by its patch of garden which acts as some sort of 'cordon sanitaire' that keeps the general public at bay. To speak literally the pavements and streets on an estate are as public as they are anywhere else. But whereas in St. Ann's they were public in the sense that they belonged to everybody, on the estates that are public in the sense that they belong to nobody.

Our Clifton housewife, who fears that her behaviour would be questioned if she dallied by the garden-gate, understands that beyond the gate lies No-Man's Land. No one lingers in No-Man's Land.

However keenly the new gardens are cultivated, and with whatever pleasure people have expanded into the more ample framework of Estate life, the informal networks of human contacts which reached over everyone in the old neighbourhoods have been radically changed. No doubt this influences memory, when people are safely removed from the disadvantages of slum life.

3. *Formal Networks*

When we interviewed the original sample of people in our first St. Ann's survey, we found just under a quarter of them belonged to trade unions, nearly 28% to a church, and less than 5% to a political party. We lost some of our original respondents, but of those we traced, 23% had been union members back in 1968. However, a lot of people had joined up in the intervening time, and union membership had increased to 35% by 1976. Political membership had also increased, but only fractionally, by a matter of 1%. Church membership had declined, to 16%. Other organisations, however, had fared better, with a positive boom in membership of various formal social organisations.

Twelve per cent now belonged to a tenants' organisation other than SATRA, which has a membership of 5% of our sample. No doubt in part this increase in support for tenant representation was due to the greatly increased sense of sharing common problems which comes from having a single landlord. Back in St. Ann's the patchwork of tenure was quite extraordinarily complicated, with numerous small landlords holding one or two houses, and very few owning substantial numbers. Many people paid their rent to an estate agent, and could not even name the owner of their property. But on the new estates, there was only one address for all complaints, the Corporation. Furthermore, however critical its tenants might be, the Corporation was always in some degree responsive to complaints, so that there was some real point in organising to press them. Back in St. Ann's we frequently met apathy engendered by acute frustration, as when one lady told us that she and her neighbour had got together to ask the rent man whether they might be allowed to paint their front doors, "if we buy the paint ourselves". "I'll have to ask, but I doubt it" he had replied. His doubts proved justified, since the landlord in question owned other houses in the terrace, and had no wish to stimulate any aesthetic sense (or any desire for rudimentary weatherproofing) among his less enterprising clients.

Six per cent of our sample now belonged to pensioners' clubs, and almost a fifth of our families numbered among their members young people in a youth club. Ten per cent also belonged to a sports club. These patterns of allegiance are greatly more developed than those we had recorded back in 1967/68, while people lived in undoubtedly the more informal community of the old redevelopment area. Easy informality, however, is probably not the only reason why people in the old slum were less prone to join clubs and societies than they now are, out on suburban estates. After all, St. Ann's was adjacent to all the City-centre amenities, many of which now seem rather remote to at least a proportion of our rehoused population.

VI Money Problems

1. *Attitudes to Income and Wealth*

So far our discussion has been confined to the immediate experiences and responses of our rehoused sample, and our emphasis has been very much on the housing itself.

But for the sample population themselves, rehousing was a major and irreversible transformation of their lives, with immediate implications which stretch far beyond the new home to embrace such vital interests as children's schooling, family shopping habits and patterns of expenditure. Rehousing is a physical and social uprooting, which puts the rehoused into quite new social situations, forces them to form new social relationships, often to alter their employment. In short, new experiences and altered circumstances may come to be reflected in an altered appreciation of one's social position, and may produce revised judgements about one's social world. One such dimension which we were anxious to re-explore was the sense in which people felt that their general economic position was appropriate and acceptable. Might it not be the case that a physical removal could stimulate consumer appetites and aspirations that were discouraged in the old slum? Might it generate new and more ambitious yardsticks for comparison in a competitive economic system? Might it significantly alter people's perceptions of what they deem normal and acceptable, or influence the critical judgements people make about the existing distribution of income, wealth and consumer goods?

Our interest in this particular set of attitudes was heightened by some of the insights that we had gained in our surveys of the late '60s. To begin with, it was then our experience that notions about wealth almost invariably took the form of assessments of regular income. The idea of ownership of capital very seldom entered into the calculations made by the families to whom we talked; a handful of people thought that ownership of "a car and a house" was a badge of wealth, but almost everyone spoke of "wealth" in terms of a steady weekly income.

This, in itself, is not particularly surprising; nearly all our respondents were people with little direct experience of capital ownership of any kind. Even the handful who owned their own homes would not have found that a particularly economically enriching circumstance. For the overwhelming majority of St. Ann's people, wealth or riches was a matter of disposable cash in hand, and cash in hand was very much a matter of immediate income-earning capacity. What was at first surprising, however, was the very modest level of earning capacity that was felt to constitute wealth. At the time the average weekly wage of an adult male was £20 6s. 0d., a fact which received considerable press and media attention, and must have been fairly generally known. Yet more than 17% of the St. Ann's dwellers whom we interviewed at about that time saw an income of £25 per week as constituting riches. (And this proportion increased to over a fifth of those who were then living on the poverty line.) This seemed to be a very modest sum, although many of our respondents must have felt that they were no more likely to achieve that small sum than any larger figure. If wealth is always just beyond one's grasp, then £25 was, for many, an entirely appropriate sum to bear in mind.

In the intervening years, inflation of both prices and wages has soared: whatever belief people may have had in the value of money has been totally eroded. One might imagine that assessments of wealth might well have inflated equally rapidly. In fact this is hardly the case. At the time our sample was reinterviewed in 1976, average male weekly earnings had reached £70.00, and there was every indication at the time of continued rapid inflation of wages and prices. How, in this very different social and economic context, was "wealth" to be assessed? In fact, no differently. Wealth was still defined in terms of immediate earning capacity and more than a fifth of our sample put that weekly sum at £60; substantially below the current average earnings. Almost four-fifths of our sample put the sum at £100 or less.

At first sight, then, the aspirations of these newly housed people had remained, at any rate financially, modest. Yet for all that there had been changes in outlook on money matters, and some of these are very interesting. First of all, although people did not put a greedy threshold on what they thought "wealth" to be, we got a number of rather strong indications that they tended to be more dissatisfied in 1976 than they had been a decade earlier. To begin with, only half those interviewed thought their income was "enough to live on" in 1976, although during our earlier enquiries 60% had said it was sufficient. Of course, rents are much higher in many council houses than they were for the demolished properties: and it is then common for people to incur higher bills, not only for transport to work or school, but also for electricity or heating, furniture and the household equipment which will fit a modern house, but could never have been accommodated in some of the older derelict ones. For many the move to a new house will have required funds for both investment in new goods, and to meet recurrent bills, some of which would necessarily and inflation apart have been substantially higher.

Much the same pattern emerges from a subjective scale; respondents were asked to describe themselves as rich, comfortable, hard-pressed or poor. On neither occasion did many people describe themselves as either rich or poor. But the second enquiry reveals that the group of "hard-pressed" had increased from 28% to 36% of the total. Clearly such a change of judgement could easily result from an expansion of felt needs, from an increased appetite for goods and services stimulated perhaps by the change of house. But it would be pious to assume that such a growth of "need", if it has really taken place, has been a painless business.

A sense of being hard-pressed could also be a small part or reflection of a much larger and ultimately more significant shift of social attitudes. Once again we have some evidence to suggest that opinion has become considerably more egalitarian, and that egalitarian sentiment is perceived to embrace other people from quite different and much more privileged social milieu.

When we compare responses to a query, first made in 1968: "Do you think wages should be more equal?", we find the following significant shift of attitude.

Table VI:1
Do you think wages should be more equal?
(responses of whole population)

	1968	1976
Yes	55%	63%
No	31%	24%
Don't Know	14%	13%

Equalitarianism had by 1976 increased quite markedly, although of course this particular question implies a comparison by wage-earners with other wage-earners, and thus restricts the meaning of the answer we received, suggesting very strongly that people fell that *working-class* incomes ought to be more equal. When the enquiry is extended to embrace other incomes, particularly incomes *outside* the working-class, we got an even sharper reaction, which seems to show a quite powerful growth of class feeling. We asked whether people thought that top people were adequately paid, grading their replies into three categories.

Table VI:2
Top People's Pay (responses of whole population)

	1968	1976
Too Much	37%	63%
Enough	6%	19%
Too little	3%	3%
Don't Know	54%	15%

Back in 1968, more than half our respondents did not offer any opinion on this matter. By 1976, 85% of the people had an opinion, and the numbers believing top people to be overpaid had increased dramatically, from less than two-fifths to more than three-fifths of the whole sample interviewed. Further, during the interval between the two enquiries, the meaning of the word "enough", in this context, had been somewhat modified, partly because there had been a prolonged discussion in the media about whether top management was under-rewarded in Britain, and much more because phase one of the Labour Government's pay policy had set a ceiling of £8,000 per annum on those incomes which qualified for any increase at all. Opinion on these matters in our sample of families was becoming clearer and sharper. Back in 1967, only 30% had thought that there should be a top limit on incomes. But in 1976, almost half were in favour of such a restriction. At the same time, because fewer people were uncertain in 1976, the number of opponents of restriction also increased, from 13% to 31%. To be sure, the then recent pay policy had not restricted the *size* of top incomes, merely seeking to control their *increase*. But since half our interviewees wished to see limits on the actual amount of such payments, and only 3% thought top people were underpaid, it is clear that this particular component of the social contract evoked some support among them. Taken together, it seems clear that these figures show that people were making more critical estimates of the overall distribution of income between different social classes, as well as supporting the idea of rather more equality within their own reference groups.

It is an interesting speculation how far rehousing contributed to these shifts of opinion. Of course, our families had not only moved house between 1967 and 1976: they had all lived through the national argument about trade unions and the Industrial Relations Acts, through miners' strikes and the downfall of the Heath administration in 1974, so that it would be very difficult to identify any one agent as causing this apparent hardening of class awareness. But rehousing, precisely because it was an unsettling experience, may have helped to shake some people out of ready acceptance of the status quo. It may have helped to open their eyes to all sorts of possibilities that would have appeared quite fanciful in the slum, and may have encouraged a much more critical appraisal of the circumstances of their own recent past, which could then have meshed in with the altogether more turbulent public moods of the '70s.

2: Trade union members and community attitudes

It is worthwhile to examine in greater detail the attitudes of the 35% of our sample who now belong to trade unions. First, we should note that nationally, in 1976 52.2% of the employed population belonged to trade unions, which proportion represented an increase of slightly less than 10% on the 1967 figures. Recruitment among resettled St. Ann's residents thus ran in front of the national rate, since our sample's union membership had gone up by 12%. When we sought to measure attitudes which were relevant to this change, it will be recalled that back in 1968, when asked if their income was "enough" 60% of those we later interviewed for a second time had replied that it was. Trade unionists among this group had given much the same answers as other people, (although in the wider sample available in the 1968 enquiry there had been differences between their responses and those of non-unionists). What was striking in 1976 was that while those "satisfied" among non-union members had shrunk to 54% of the total, less than half of the trade unionists (48%) replied that their incomes were "enough". When asked to rate themselves on a five-point scale saying whether they were wealthy, quite well-off, comfortable, hard-pressed, or poor, one-third of the trade unionists, and nearly two-fifths of the others at work, replied that they were now "hard pressed". In each case these answers reflected a sharp increase in readiness to complain of need, and among trade unionists this readiness had doubled.

Alongside this sharpening of discontent with their personal position, there appeared a growing sentiment of class distinction. When we asked three questions calculated to reveal such responses, the results all showed a marked increase in equalitarian sentiments. Asked first whether *wages* should be more equal (that is to say, working-class incomes should be more evenly distributed) three-fifths of both union and non-union members replied "yes", as compared with just over half the non-unionists, and just under half the unionists, in 1968. But when asked whether top people's pay was too much, 62% now thought it was, compared to 34% who had believed it so during the earlier enquiry. When we came to see whether there should, in our sample's opinion, be "a top limit on pay", no less than 80% of our trade unionists now agreed that there should, as compared with less than one-third of the 1967 replies. Some non-unionists were now for more radical in this issue: overall, 47% as opposed to an earlier 27% now favoured such a limit.

Without wishing to stretch this evidence too far, it seems plain that, following their move, our population were more prone to join formal organisations of different kinds, more likely than the national average worker to join up with a trade union for the first time, more equalitarian in their outlooks, more aware of economic pressures on their own budgets, and more ready to see the imposition of restrictions on wealthier people. In short, rehousing had not assimilated people into what are commonly alleged to be "middle-class" attitudes, but had, if anything, somewhat reinforced their "working-class" outlook.

Yet, noticeably, while unions had benefited from this hardening of opinion, the Labour Party had not gained any serious number of individual members.

3. *Ownership of Consumer Durables*

The move from an old, cramped, and sub-standard house, into one that was considerably more modern, spacious, and equipped with such standard household amenities as a hot-water system, a bathroom and power-sockets in most rooms, represented in itself a powerful alteration in personal circumstances. Some delighted reactions to these changes have already been documented in some detail. But as important was the alteration in perspectives about the possibilities for yet further improvements, represented in the purchase of a range of consumer durable goods.

Not only does a council house offer more space than a confined terrace slum, or one of the artisan properties on the fringes of old St. Ann's: but all the commercial and cultural pressures combine to goad people into seeking the comforts of modern living. While one lived in a small house, ill-equipped with power-points, then a whole range of household electrical items, whether labour-saving (such as vacuum-cleaners, washing machines), or leisure-enhancing (such as hi-fi sets) were equally impractical, even where one had the means to purchase them. Insofar as the changed housing removed the practical obstacles, so the consumer desires could develop and grow, powerfully reinforced no doubt by the advertising pressures of the media, as well as the social pressures and expectations generated within each person's personal, family and social environment.

If practicality and cupidity have played their part, so has a new pattern of necessity.

Some household items have become a bit more than merely desirable, once one moves away from a crowded city centre to a peripheral estate, where one is far from the Bendix, or the municipal washhouses which were used by so many of the women in the old St. Ann's. Moreover, if daily chores such as washing the laundry, are now "privatised" through the purchase of a washing-machine, it does not seem unreasonable to assume that the move to new housing has made people generally more home-centred, at any rate in their spending habits.

But even this is rather more complicated a matter than it might at first sight appear to be. All consumer durables involve expenditure, for their purchase, their running, their maintenance and repair and ultimately their replacement. But some purchases rest upon a foundation of earlier purchases. No one buys a vacuum cleaner unless they have at least started out on the carpeting of their house. Our survey did not explore other kinds of purchases in detail, but it seems reasonable to assume that the need for, and of course the costs of curtaining, furnishing and keeping up the new houses are all larger than was the case in the old terraces. Rents, of course, are higher, and so are heating costs, at any rate in the houses of the new

St. Ann's, which shares a controversial and expensive district heating scheme.

A clear majority of those we asked said that the St. Ann's district heating system worked "badly" or "very badly". Most people said they did not like the system and even those who said they approved of it were conscious that it had "problems". These problems were not overwhelmingly associated with the cost of the scheme, since more than half our respondents thought it was "value for money".

For all these reasons, then, we anticipated that our sample would show a marked alteration in the possession of household goods. And a simple comparison of the two samples bears this out; 92 families owned washing machines in 1976, as compared to 74 a decade earlier. Distance from the corner shop might account for the even larger increase in refrigerator ownership, from 24 to 108. Hoovers had proliferated to 102 from 67, and by 1976 46 people had bought or rented colour television sets, while only one family had previously owned such a set in 1967. TV ownership in general, including both colour and black-and-white sets, had increased from 130 in 1967 to 140 in 1976.

Almost everyone had been to the shops. Only 15 people told us that they had not been compelled to make any new purchases as a result of their move: but 80 had bought new furniture, 60 had purchased electrical goods, 100 had needed carpeting, and 55 had been involved in other unspecified outlay. All but three of those people we traced in 1976 had found themselves paying higher rents: 86 people had greater fares-bills, and 121 were spending appreciably more on heating.

But there is one arresting fact which throws some doubt on the picture of increasing affluence that this suggests and offers, perhaps, a hint of the underlying and hard economic choices that have to be made.

At a time when people were being compelled to make what were often considerably longer journeys to work, when many had been moved to relatively remote estates, several miles from the City Centre, ill-served by public transport, at a time in short when many people might need the use of a car more than they had previously, leave alone any shift in general social expectations about car ownership, car ownership in fact showed a net decline from 34 to 29 householders. No doubt this reflects the ever-increasing costs of buying, maintaining and running a car which have inexorably squeezed some of our small sample out of the market-place.

This thought encourages the search for comparative data. Motor cars apart, do these large increases in ownership of consumer durables reflect a "normalisation" of the actual life-standards of the rehoused population? How far has our population, which was beyond doubt quite spectacularly deprived in 1966, been able to catch up with the rest of the country?

If we compare the national and regional patterns of ownership of the same articles, we get a clear picture of how far this same population has still to move in order to catch up with everyone else. Table VI:3 is based on data published in the Family

Expenditure Survey for 1976: it shows that the former citizens of St. Ann's are only level of the rest of the population in one respect: between them they own about the same proportion of TV sets. (Sampling errors could easily reverse the tiny lead given to our groupings in the last line of this table, so narrow is the gap between the figures.) In all other respects the Nottingham survey deals with people who are worse off than the inhabitants of the region as a whole. The declining figure of car ownership actually reveals that the population of the East Midlands as a whole and even of the UK nationally is more than two and a half times better-favoured than are our rehoused sample.

Table VI:3
Households with certain durable goods (%)

	Rehoused from St.Ann's	East Midlands	UK
	1976	1975-6	1975-6
Car	20.6	57.1	56.1
Washing Machine	66.0	81.4	72.1
Refrigerator	76.7	85.2	86.7
TV	96.4	95.4	95.2

As we pointed out in our original report, such questions as we asked do leave out a great deal of matter about which we might well be curious. "Owners of certain consumer goods" are a category which conceals wide qualitative variations. Some goods are new from the store: many are second, third or fifth hand, or simply rather old. Some represent large debts on hire-purchase, while others have been painlessly acquired for cash. Without being able to go into these matters of acquisition, we have by no means exhausted the scope for enquiry about how well off the rehoused population is, by comparison with everyone else.

VII The virtues of council housing

If, as we saw in Chapter V, the redevelopment of St. Ann's has actually been followed by a strengthening of the extended family, then we are bound to pay some special attention to those housing policies which may have been conducive to this effect. We have already discussed the limits within which the rather remarkable statistic (a rise from 56% to 82% of respondents having family members living "nearby") should be interpreted. Even though we make every allowance for special explanations, it is quite clear that the elaborate processes of choice which have been involved in this rehousing operation would have been quite inconceivable had the Corporation not been a landlord on a vast scale, within whose empires lay easy permutations of exchange of houses, a widespread choice of locations and addresses, and a rather simple set of mechanisms for exercising such choices.

Yet, in recent years, this freedom and flexibility has not received its due recognition: on the contrary, there has developed (in the minds of some) the curious notion that the general public welfare would be better served, as would the private interest of tenants and householders, if this stock of publicly-owned and administered housing were to be sold off, enlarging the privately owned sector of housing, and enabling groups of people who have always rented their housing to enjoy both the benefits and responsibilities of private ownership. That, for people living on small incomes, these benefits might be dubious and their concomitant responsibilities heavy, has not deterred the advocates of this change. From time to time over the past few years some local housing authorities have made strenuous endeavours to realise it. The leaders of the Greater London Council announced their intention to divest themselves of the entire GLC housing stock in an operation which was then described as "the sale of the century", while Nottingham's own civic leaders until May 1979 offered for sale every council house that became vacant, again indicating their desire to sell off the entire municipal pool of housing. A combination of circumstances, including problems of mortgage finance as well as the hesitation of potential customers (whether sitting tenants or not) who showed indifferent zeal in responding to the Council's offer, has ensured that this rather ideological prescription has had only limited impact. The issue is not by any means resolved however, and it may therefore be worthwhile to relate the findings of this survey to the more general discussion of public sector housing.

In September 1979 the Nottingham City Council owned approximately 54,000 council dwellings, including not only purpose-built council houses and flats, but also numbers of privately-built houses which had been bought by the Corporation for different reasons. Some had been taken over because they were in possible redevelopment areas, (usually but not always old and relatively poor quality properties) while others had been bought new from private developers during previous economic recessions and times of difficulty for the building trade. The council had also itself built a certain number of houses especially for re-sale, having at the time of purchase no intention of letting them in the normal way. At the beginning of the '70s council policy was to encourage the sale of its housing stock, but this policy was subsequently halted.

It was reintroduced in May 1976. Between that date and September 1979, the council had sold 5,468 houses, or about 10% of its remaining stock. Up to one third of these sales were from the stocks of houses deliberately built for sale, or taken over upon completion from private developers. The remainder were sold out of the conventional stock of houses originally built for letting under the traditional rules governing public housing projects. This sales policy has been controversial and has been the subject not only of heated debate, but of various reversals and switches. Broadly, when in recent times the Conservatives have held office they have favoured selling the housing stock, and this policy has been threatened whenever Labour has become the majority Party. The advent of Labour Control, or to be more accurate, a particular crisis-point when an industrial dispute hit the building trade sometime soon after the changeover, saw one such major change. Another followed when a renewed political switch took place in 1976, as we have seen, re-introducing selling on a heavier scale, with greater determination.

Nationally, there was a boom in council house sales under the Heath administration, followed by an interruption between 1974 and 1976, and then a lesser upturn after that date:

VII:1
Council House Sales 1970-8

	Local Authorities	New Towns	National Total	Nottingham
1970	6,231	223	6,454	
1971	16,851	2,755	19,606	
1972	45,058	15,603	60,661	2,600
1973	33,720	7,254	40,974	
1974	4,153	653	4,806	
1975	2,089	175	2,264	—
1976	4,582	62	4,644	
1977	12,019	330	12,349	5,468*
1978	28,540	360	28,900	
1979	NK	NK	NK	NK

But in Nottingham this cycle has followed a reverse pattern, with something over two and a half thousand sales in the first boom, and five and a half thousand in the later one. This remarkable upswing attracted widespread national curiosity and investigation, culminating in a programme for Thames Television by its documentary unit, *TV Eye*. Thames sent a Mr and Mrs T.V. Eye to buy council houses in Nottingham, and they

---

*plus 138 offers accepted but not yet sold.

proved embarrassingly successful. Ostensibly, the policy of sales was restricted by the circumstance that only persons on the council's 8,000-long waiting list were eligible to buy. But the Thames researchers quickly found that joining the waiting list was a five-minute formality, which involved no difficulties whatever. As the local newspaper reported:

> "The programme . . . sets out to show that it's possible to buy a council house in Nottingham within a day of arriving.
>
> Reporter Mike Walsh, from ITV'S *TV Eye* visited Nottingham to investigate the sale of council houses. Using the alias Terence Victor Eye he told the council he was moving from Hull and wanted to buy a house for cash.
>
> Council houses are only sold to people on the city's 8,000 long waiting list, sitting tenants or residents from clearance areas. But on the day Mr T.V. Eye started discussions with the council he claims he was given a form to fill in for the waiting list and — after paying his £5 deposit — the key to a house in Thistledown Road."

The City Council threatened legal action to stop the transmission of the programme, and its leader sought police intervention against the journalists involved. Unfortunately, Nottingham is not in Bulgaria, and the constabulary displayed a remarkably determined lack of interest in the causes of the annoyance suffered by their City fathers.

There are two particular aspects of this issue that merit further consideration. First, we may reasonably entertain doubts about some of the freedoms allegedly conferred by owner-occupation, particularly among people with few resources of capital or savings, and with very modest amounts of discretionary income. The most obvious "freedom" involved concerns the owner's discretion to manage his property as he thinks fit, to decorate when he likes, in whatever colours he likes, to make alterations to the structure of their property (subject, of course, to any general planning restrictions), in short to do what he wants with his own. For most people in practice, this grand-sounding liberty is quickly reduced to an expensive and time-consuming responsibility for the maintenance and upkeep of the property. To be sure, poorer people do have one discretion in respect of such matters: they may always choose to delay works of renovation and maintenance until the expense involved has become quite unavoidable.

The other "freedom" is even more illusory: the chance to see your investment grow in value, enabling you upon resale of the propery to secure a substantial tax-free capital gain. There are a number of problems here, apart from the fact that, unless one contemplates living in a tent, most people who sell one house are obliged to purchase another, so that their capital gain from the one will be absorbed by the inflated price of the other. But moving house is an extremely expensive business, involving prolonged and costly negotation with a tight network of professional advisors. Starting with estate agents, solicitors, and chartered surveyors, the house purchaser often then runs a gauntlet of mortgage-men and insurance brokers, as well, all of whom require fees, commissions, honoraria and other emoluments. Throughout this painful and nerve-wracking process the client discovers that the flow of resources is strictly one-way: outwards.

As if that were not enough, the housing market itself is a volatile one, moving rapidly from booms to recessions, embroiling one in never-ending and closely interlocked chains of purchases and sales which can explode in one's face without warning, necessarily involving further delays and, of course, expense.

The upshot is that while mobility in the housing market remains a technical possibility for owner-occupiers, in practice it is only slightly to be preferred to divorce in its capacity to impose personal strain upon everyone impartially, unless one is protected by a considerable margin of spare cash.

In contrast to this, considerable, very tangible and almost cost-free benefits may derive from a large stock of publicly owned houses.

We are not here concerned with the general controversy about public ownership of housing, but with the particular effect that a large public sector may have upon the thriving, or otherwise, of family connections. What makes choice feasible, and allows family members the possibility of an option to move closer (or for that matter, if they wish, further away) from their relatives, is the fact that the Council owns many houses in many localities. If everyone owned a house, such movement would still be more difficult, if only because of the complex protocol involved in selling and buying new properties in the private market, which far outweighs in difficulty the process of transfer from one publicly rented house to another. When large numbers of people do not own either a house or the resources which must be necessarily involved in purchasing one, this mobility is even more impeded, unless one common authority exists, which may facilitate exchanges precisely to the extent that it has houses in every area. The housing market in privately rented properties is even less "free" than the labour market, in that various acts of social legislation have, for very good reasons, laid down numerous obstacles to the free conduct of operations which inevitably render difficult movement between one area and another. It is for these reasons that widespread public investment in council housing may indeed strengthen the extended family, which is otherwise threatened by innumerable social and commercial pressures quite apart from the institution of slum clearance.

This of course is not to say that we should be complacent about the management of local authority housing. There are no doubt many long-overdue reforms here, reducing the weight of bureaucracy and extending council tenants' rights. A much more adventurous approach to housing administration, involving experiments with housing co-operatives, tenant control of estates, and encouraging more effective self-help and communal participation and involvement, would greatly humanize what is all too often, a dully unimaginative albeit competent management. These desirable reforms, however, can only take place within a large and dynamic public housing sector.

Few, if any of the criticisms levelled at local authorities will be met by a single-minded and one-sided commitment to owner-occupation for all, whether they like it or not.

The Nottingham authority has sold to sitting tenants 1,941 of the 5,468 houses disposed of during the period 1976-9. But if the deeds of all these houses had been transferred only to present residents, this would still represent a 10% diminution of the total council-owned housing stock, and thus of the potential area of choice and exchange in which the extended family might still hope to reassert itself.

The argument against the sale of council houses normally turns on a variety of public issues. On the one side, it is commonly claimed that sales mean "poor law" housing, social segregation of the disadvantaged, and in the end a diminution of the public capacity to meet real housing needs.[1] On the other, it is argued that lost revenue and mortgage tax relief combine to deplete the public purse at both local and national levels.[2] To both these well-publicized pleas we think it appropriate to add a third: that the effect on family-life and social support networks of a wide spread of public, welfare housing estates may well be an advantage not appreciated in full until its loss registers, retrospectively, a net decline in the quality of life in Britain.

Footnotes
1. "Paying the Price of Council House Sales" in *Roof* Nov. 1978, pp.170-173.
2. "How a Council Loses on Sales" in *Roof* May 1977, pp.76-80.

Appendix

The Conduct of the Surveys

Methodology

There have been many studies of urban redevelopment schemes; most have taken some interest in the sorts of questions discussed in the body of this monograph. How rehousing is experienced, the different ways in which people react to such experience, the effects or consequences of rehousing and its impact on the formal and informal structures within which people conduct their lives: all these are important questions to which researchers have directed their attention.

What is rare, however, is to encounter research where the enquiry has first-hand and detailed knowledge about a population's attitudes, expectations and life-styles well before redevelopment occurs, which can be matched with equivalent information collected from the same people after redevelopment. We are able partially to fill that gap thanks to a rich source of data, gathered between February 1967 and June 1968 in St. Ann's, Nottingham, while redevelopment proposals were being discussed but before their implementation. This comprises extended interviews with a sample population of over 400 families living in the old St. Ann's. In the course of these interviews a great deal of factual information was gathered about the household and family structure, housing conditions, family income etc. But the interviews also discussed attitudes and feelings about these matters, and hopes and aspirations about the future in general and the redeveloped St. Ann's in particular. Much of this material has already been reported at length and published elsewhere, but this monograph will add to the published volume of data originating in the surveys of ten years ago, and will offer a fresh interpretation of some of it, in the light of new material derived from a programme of follow-up interviews carried out in the Spring of 1976.

We believe that material of this kind, whatever its many apparent shortcomings, is very rarely encountered, and may be in some respects unique. Many investigations into housing and other matters, have asked respondents to recall their feelings and attitudes, to try and remember what their views were at an earlier period in their lives; these memories are then contrasted with their current opinions. This practice is the best one can do, in the absence of a more reliable source of "before-information". At the same time, the dangers of faulty recall are so obvious that data of this kind has to be assessed with great reservations about both its completeness and its reliability. Some other enquiries have attempted to build upon earlier projects, by asking many of the same questions, but these have normally been directed to a freshly drawn sample of the population; the questions are the same but the people are not. There are few examples of a truly longitudinal survey where, after a due interval of time, the same and further questions are put to precisely the same households, whose earlier expressions of fact or opinion are already known. This is what has been attempted in the present enquiry, where we have interviewed 141 of the original families, first interviewed in 1967/68, subsequently rehoused by the local authority, and now living in another house situated anything from a few yards to six miles away from their original address.

There is no magic or mystery about the figure of 141 fresh interviews. This is the largest total that we were able to muster, and it calls for a few words of explanation. First, we shall be asked, what has happened to the larger group of 250 odd households whom we have not re-interviewed? And secondly, how representative of our original larger sample is this smaller group?

As has been indicated, we had (in 1976) a nine year old original data-base which comprised 413 interviews. This grand total was in practice reduced to 386 questionnaires through loss, damage or incomplete information. Taking these 386 households we knew that each one (allowing for a tiny handful of exceptions) had been rehoused in many cases as much as five or six years previously, and scattered over all parts of the City. The practical obstacles to tracing our original sample were obvious and daunting.

Our first consideration was that a number of

our original respondents, particularly those of advanced years, would have died in the interim. Secondly, a number of our respondents had moved out of Nottingham altogether, sometimes to other towns and cities in the UK, and sometimes to other countries.

We secured considerable help and co-operation from the City Housing Department, to whom we supplied a list of our original addresses. The Department then supplied us with the new address of the family they had rehoused from that old house in St. Ann's. We obtained in this way 283 addresses, those missing including the dead, the people who had moved completely away from the town, and some cases where the house turned out to be empty by the time the Rehousing Officer arrived. This last group consisted of tenants who made alternative arrangements of their own, whether by buying or by renting, and did not wait for public rehousing. This intriguing group of people who so quietly and effectively disappear from the registers of social research as well as from the Council's list of immediate responsibility, constitutes one of the many mysteries in the housing field. That there is a sizeable minority of people who vanish in this independent manner is a consistently observed phenomenon. But very little is known about them as a group, nor is it clear how well they cope with their housing difficulties.

In any event, we thus located 283 addresses which at that stage we believed to be the new addresses of our original sample and after due preparation the interviewing could begin. In any survey of this sort you can never hope to get a complete set of answers, as the effective total is eroded by practical difficulties in finding people, and securing their co-operation. We experienced 24 refusals to be re-interviewed and in another 20 cases were never able to establish contact with our respondents despite letters and several visits to their homes. Then we encountered cases, 18 of them, where our respondents, again mainly pensioners, had died at some time after their move and some, to us, quite new family had taken over the tenancy. In a further 5 cases we established beyond doubt that our families were not longer living either at that address, nor indeed in Nottingham, but had moved to another city, or again, (in two cases), had left the country.

Although a disappointment to us, because our possible total of completed interviews was being constantly reduced, we had expected to come across cases of these kinds, so we were not in any way surprised. What did surprise us, however, and, at times, depress us considerably, was the emergence of two other large groups of, from our viewpoint, failed interviews. In 45 cases, after an interview was successfully completed and a start had been made on the analysis of the data that had been gathered [in two interviews separated by up to 9 years], it became apparent that although the re-interviewed family had been rehoused from St. Ann's, and indeed had been rehoused from the very home that we had called on in 1967 or 1968, it was not the same family that we had interviewed in the first instance. The reasons for this curious and infuriating anomaly gradually became clear. What had happened was that our original family, for any of the reasons already noted, had moved from their old St. Ann's address at some time before the Council were proposing to rehouse them. These empty houses in St. Ann's had then been taken over by a new set of tenants, with whom of course we had no previous contact at all, and it was these tenants who were ultimately rehoused, and their new address that we obtained.

The final large group, 30 of them, were families whom we had interviewed in St. Ann's, who had been rehoused, whose new addresses we obtained but who by the time we called upon them had moved yet again. In these cases we had no reason to believe that the families had left Nottingham, indeed there was good reason to believe that they were still in the City but they had moved, or had been moved, to another address. Diligent efforts were made to trace this group but without success.

In the end then we succeeded in completing 141 interviews with families who were without question the same people we had spoken with during our earlier surveys. This was a third of our original group, and a half of those for whom we had a second address.

As part of our purpose was always to investigate changes in attitudes and feelings, as well as the more obvious changes in physical circumstances, we were naturally concerned to establish whether our 141 second interviews represented a biased or distorted sub-sample.

It is possible to answer this question with some confidence, because we were able to construct a profile of the 1967/68 population who subsequently vanished, and compare it with the 1967/68 profile of those we managed to trace and re-interview. In only one significant respect was there any substantial difference between the two profiles. That was that our 1967/68 group contained a proportion of single working male householders which was under-represented in our later group. Of course it is precisely this group of single, adult males who have the greatest geographical mobility, the greatest discretionary income relative to their requirements, and may feel the least compulsion to wait around in a visibly decaying environment. For this group, the offer of a council house or flat, while it may hold certain attractions, may not represent the compelling inducement to remain, if need be for an indefinitely long time, that it would be to the more hard-pressed family man with dependent children. Nonetheless the erosion of this group does introduce a small bias or distortion of which the reader should be aware.

Acknowledgements

This study was made possible by a small grant of money from the Nottinghamshire County Council Research Fund, which was established within the University of Nottingham in 1975 by a generous gift of the County Council. This was intended to furnish small grants to support research with a local interest. Being among the first to benefit from this source, we would like to express our appreciation to Dick Wilson, the leader of the Council at the time, whose far-sighted, generous and disinterested concern for scholarship inspired the establishment of this useful link between the University and the Local Authority.

A great part of the thankless burden of interviewing and consequent data-processing was willingly borne by a group of friends, notably Ruth Bennett, Ann Elsey, Nicola Wilkins, and most of all Mike Barr, without whose enthusiasm, dedication and subsequent prodding the work might never have been finished. As always we gladly pay tribute to our colleagues and the heads of our Departments, Professors Marsh and Stephens, not only for their constant encouragement, but also for their considerable patience. We also wish to thank all those members of the WEA who have helped us in this work ever since 1967, and the public officials who gave us invaluable advice and assistance.

Above all, however, we hope that this monograph will commend itself to its subjects, the long-suffering residents of the old St Ann's to whose many burdens was added the imposition of our own interest and curiosity. We hope that they will think it worthwhile. Needless to say, the responsibility for all judgements expressed, sound or otherwise, is ours and ours alone.